Y

THE BASICS

Christianity: The Basics is a compelling introduction to both the central pillars of the Christian faith and the rich and varied history of this most global of global religions. This book traces the development of Christianity through an exploration of some of the key beliefs, practices and emotions which have been recurrent symbols through the centuries:

- Christ, the kingdom of heaven, and sin
- Baptism, Eucharist, and prayer
- Joy, divine union, and self-denial

Encompassing the major epochs of Christian history and examining the unity and divisions created by these symbols, *Christianity: The Basics* is both a concise and comprehensive introduction to the Christian tradition.

Bruce Chilton is a leading scholar of early Christianity and Judaism and is currently Bernard Iddings Bell Professor of Religion at Bard, where he also directs the Institute of Advanced Theology. He has taught in Europe at the Universities of Cambridge, Sheffield, and Münster, and in the United States at Yale University (as the first Lillian Claus Professor of New Testament).

The Basics

CHRISTIANITY

THE BASICS

Bruce Chilton

Routledge
Taylor & Francis Group

LONDON AND NEW YORK

First published 2015
by Routledge
2 Park Square, Milton Park, Abingdon, Oxon OX14 4RN

and by Routledge
711 Third Avenue, New York, NY 10017

Routledge is an imprint of the Taylor & Francis Group, an informa business

© 2015 Bruce Chilton

British Library Cataloguing in Publication Data
A catalogue record for this book is available from the British Library

Library of Congress Cataloging in Publication Data
Chilton, Bruce.
Christianity : the basics / Bruce Chilton. -- 1 [edition].
pages cm. -- (The basics)
Includes bibliographical references and index.
 1. Christianity--Essence, genius, nature. 2. Church history. I. Title.
BT60.C49 2014
230--dc23
2014001746

ISBN: 978-0-415-53810-7 (hbk)
ISBN: 978-0-415-53809-1 (pbk)
ISBN: 978-1-315-76544-0 (ebk)

Typeset in Bembo
by Taylor & Francis Books

MIX
Paper from
responsible sources
FSC
www.fsc.org   FSC® C013604   Printed and bound by CPI Group (UK) Ltd, Croydon, CR0 4YY

CONTENTS

PREFACE

The basics of Christianity involve practices, beliefs, and moral engagements. Each of these features has evolved over time, so that there is no such thing as a single set of Christian basics that has always remained, without change. Yet over time key formulations of how to worship, what to believe, and right action in society have emerged as points of reference for believers across cultures and periods. These are the basics we encounter in this volume.

In order to understand them, two principles of study need to be observed. The first is historical, and the second theoretical.

An historical perspective enables us to see how each basic emerged in its own time, either as an articulation of a principle that had long been at work, or as a fresh development that believers from that time onward felt compelled to take into account. To accommodate the need to deal with over two millennia of evolution—ranging from the period of the Judaism out of which Christianity emerged to the present—chronological stages are set out, chapter by chapter. Each epoch has contributed its basics, not necessarily in the sense of universally accepted features, but as elements of faith that have demanded consideration and response.

The definition of each epoch involves the second, theoretical principle alongside an historical lens. Religions do not randomly change their practices, beliefs, and moral imperatives. Rather, all three are coordinated in a system, so that each feature influences the others, and is affected by them. Christianity shares this systemic character with other religions.

For the purpose of the comparative study of religion, religious systems are approached along the lines of ritual, meaning, and ethics. In the Introduction, each of these terms is explained further. (As the volume unfolds, some of the secondary literature is mentioned, where theoretical discussion outside the purview of this series may be pursued.) But we can say provisionally that "ritual" refers to the agreed activities that people in society learn in order to relate commonly to one another and to the central values they share. "Meaning" involves how those values are articulated into a coherent view of the purpose of life in society, and often beyond society. (Typically, meaning involves a conception of the divine, but there are religious systems that resist postulation of God.) Finally, ethics is the actionable face of a religious system, where a person's engagement with daily life articulates religion in immediate terms.

By approaching the basics of Christianity as a religious system that evolves through history, both their context and their significance will make it plain what makes them indispensable. At the same time, a theoretical approach that assesses Christianity as scholars of religion might approach any system means the analysis might benefit, not only practitioners, but all those who wish to understand how the world's largest religion has grown, evolved, and shaped the sensibilities of its adherents.

Epiphany 2014

INTRODUCTION

The most obvious basic of Christianity is that its foundation is Christ. The Greek term *khristos* means that Jesus of Nazareth is "anointed," the person specially chosen by God. But anointed in what sense? Is Jesus chosen in the same way that the king of Israel was? Anointing designated the Israelite king; for this reason he could be called the Messiah (*mashiach* in Hebrew). Some of Jesus' followers during his time viewed him as "anointed" in this sense, but others saw him as a specially designated prophet or teacher. (The address "rabbi," the most common title of Jesus in the Gospels, highlights his teaching role). "Son of God" is another designation, and it raises questions about Jesus' birth that remain open. Even as that title has proven mysterious, "son of man" also appears, and is used by Jesus in reference to himself.

CHRIST OR MESSIAH

Christ derives from the word *khristos* in Greek and means someone who is anointed. The equivalent in Hebrew is *mashiach*, which gives us the English word **Messiah**. In the Hebrew Bible, a person might be anointed with olive oil as a routine matter, to cleanse the skin or care for a wound, and

scented oil was a luxury. But anointing might also designate someone as a king, a prophet, or a priest, so the term
itself came to imply religious status. When belief in Jesus
and his resurrection spread outside the land of Israel to
the city of Antioch, non-Jewish people were attracted to the
faith in large numbers. In an attempt to describe this new
group of believers, which did not fit into conventions of
Jewish or pagan groups, people in Antioch began to call
them "Partisans of Christ" (*khristianoi*; Acts 11:26). The
term carried political overtones, much as today followers of
a leader are named after him or her by adding the suffix
"-ite" to the leader's name. The label "Christian" began its
long history as an outsiders' name that tried to put the
movement in its place by calling attention to its attempt to
exalt its humiliated founder.

How Jesus was identified—by himself, by his followers, and by
people outside his movement—is a fascinating question. During the
course of this book, we will see several identifications as they were
deployed in their original contexts. But Christian believers, whether
ancient or modern, have not practiced their faith by beginning each
day asking about which title should be applied to Jesus. Rather,
they have met the challenges of their times and discovered their
hopes by seeing Jesus within the whole tapestry of their faith,
relating him to themselves and to God.

Understanding the basics of Christianity means seeing how the
religion unfolded in time, producing features such as prayers,
creeds, forms of worship, doctrines, and social movements that
emerged and have proven themselves vital over a period of two
thousand years. As in the case of other religions, Christianity relates
three kinds of human activity to one another: ritual, ethics, and
philosophy. These activities can, of course, also be seen and studied
separately. That is why religions are powerful social and historical
forces—they combine social relations and activities that can exist
independently. Religions put them together into a mutually reinforcing
system.

Religions involve ritual activity: a set of communal actions in
which each participant understands the role to be played and the

sequence of acts to be followed. Rituals need not be religious; they are a common part of secular experience, ranging from a small elementary-school graduation to the inauguration of a political leader. In the case of religion, rituals relate to two other kinds of activity, ethical and philosophical.

Together with rituals, religions concern ethics, how people should behave, whether in public or in private. Questions such as who can marry whom, what professions are acceptable, and when the responsibilities of being an adult need to be taken up are all ethical concerns that religions typically address.

Any one kind of activity can influence another in the setting of religion. A ritual of passage at puberty, for example, might mark the moment that a child is viewed as an adult, so that the relationship between ritual and ethical activity is obvious. But in addition to these ritual and ethical concerns, religions also involve a third dimension of activity, that of meaning or practical philosophy: religions tell participants *why* they do what they do, and even why they exist, in much the same way that philosophies do.

Just as ritual may influence ethics, so changes of meaning can alter the other kinds of activity. Precisely when a child becomes an adult, for example, is a philosophical determination that is made differently in different cultures, and Christianity over time has developed different views, with coordinating ethical and ritual adjustments.

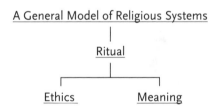

A General Model of Religious Systems

|

Ritual

|

Ethics   Meaning

This book traces how ritual, ethics, and meaning have produced basic features of Christianity over time. Their interactions have not only determined what a given feature, such as a creed, is but also why it emerged when it did and how it influenced the religion as a whole.

Historical development forms an important aspect of this work, for the obvious reason that Christianity has changed over time. By paying attention to how ritual, ethics, and meaning interact, we will build an understanding of both continuities and differences—sometimes revolutionary shifts—within the Christian tradition.

But history needs to be our guide for a more subtle and fundamental reason. Christianity did not simply emerge out of one person's contribution: not even Jesus (or Paul, as is sometimes suggested) invented the new faith. Rather, the earliest framers of Christianity consciously engaged with the Judaism of their time, and in that engagement they both changed the religious system they inherited and fashioned a new religion.

For that reason, "The Basics of Jesus" (Chapter 1), with its focus on the origins of Christianity, will deal with the fundamental system of Judaism in the first century, and how the events of that time and the vision of Jesus produced what practitioners of the new faith, casual observers, and enemies alike came to regard as a new religion.

Christianity unfolded in a hostile environment within the Roman Empire. Because the system was new, a recent superstition (as the Romans said), rather than an ancient tradition, Christians were at best marginalized and at times actively subjected to violence. Their preaching that the Spirit that came from Jesus transcended conventional barriers between people and classes and united humanity in the single hope of resurrection seemed to undermine Roman conceptions of political rule and social status. Yet the teachers of "Catholic, Orthodox Basics" (Chapter 2) set out the claims of the new faith so vigorously that Christianity in the fourth century found itself *at the center of power* in a political machine that once rejected it. This transition, a matter of consensus by the Middle Ages, proved to be the most radical in the history of the Church.

As long as the center of the Roman Empire held, until 1453 in the case of its capital city (Constantinople), Christianity enjoyed not only preference, but also a degree of influence over policy and society unparalleled in its history. But the fall of Rome to Alaric in the West (in 410 CE) meant that Europe confronted the challenge of fragmentation during the Middle Ages; that has molded the character of Western Catholicism ever since. Although Eastern Christianity (that is, Orthodoxy) could rely on a center of support for a thousand years longer than the West could, invasions from Asia and Turkey destabilized imperial authority, and the expansion of Orthodoxy into new lands, Slavic and Russian, raised questions of the relationship to new political powers that had not been faced before. In both East and West, Christianity needed to frame a view of how the faith could save believers in environments that were so hostile and unpredictable that they called Christ's triumph over evil into question. "Basics in the Middle Ages" (Chapter 3) contributed both practices and attitudes that still define the current conception of the faith.

The great religious divides between Catholic and Protestant in the West have their origin in the following period. Both those wings of what had been a united Western Christendom developed an increasing distance from Orthodoxy in the East, which in turn produced its own articulation of classic religious foundations. In this, as in every period that will concern us, the roots of new forms are to be found in older sources, but the fact of profound controversy shows up in deep, sometimes deadly debates over how Christianity should be defined and practiced. The Church inherited "Reformation and Enlightenment Basics" (Chapter 4) that continue to involve polemics and self-examination.

Modernity, with its pluralism of religion and increasingly secular views of the nature of political power, poses a challenge—some would say a threat—to Christianity. But the policies of tolerance that permitted pluralism, and the view of government as separate from religion, in fact stem, as we will see, from the ferment of discussion that followed the Reformation and the Counter-Reformation. Today's world, different though it is from previous epochs, is no less implicated in the rituals, ethics, and account of meaning that Christianity has offered since its birth. "The Basics of Modern Christianity" (Chapter 5) play their part in defining the global scene in dialogue with the many alternative modernities of our time.

SUMMARY

In this introduction we have seen:

- What is involved in studying any religion, a system that relates ritual, ethics, and meaning;

- That Christianity during its two-thousand year history has seen changes in those three concerns;
- That the religion emerged with distinctive practices and beliefs during successive periods: origins (the first century), classic foundations (between the second and the ninth centuries), consolidation (in the Middle Ages), critical redefinition (during the Reformation and the Enlightenment), and modernity.

From this point of view, we can encounter and analyze the basics of Christianity.

TIMELINE

CHAPTER 1: THE BASICS OF JESUS

4 BCE   The death of Herod the Great.
2 CE   The birth of Jesus.
21 CE   The death of John the Baptist.
31 CE   Jesus' occupation of the Temple.
32 CE   The death of Jesus, and his followers' experience of his resurrection.

CHAPTER 2: CATHOLIC, ORTHODOX BASICS

45 CE   In Antioch followers of Jesus are for the first time called "Christians."
46 CE   A meeting of the apostles in Jerusalem resolves that Gentile believers need not keep the custom of male circumcision.
52 CE   An ancillary meeting places ritual requirements on Gentile believers. When taken together with the session of 46 CE, as in Acts 15, the meetings are known as the Jerusalem Council.
53–57   Paul writes his major letters, Galatians, Corinthians, and Romans.
62 CE   Death of James, Jesus' elder half-brother, in Jerusalem.

64 CE	Deaths of Peter and Paul in Rome.
66 CE	The refusal of Caesar's payment for sacrifice in the Temple brings on the Roman military response to the Jewish revolt.
70–73 CE	The burning of the Temple by the Roman troops under Titus; the composition of Mark's Gospel in Rome; the end of the revolt against Rome in Palestine.
80 CE	The composition of Matthew's Gospel, in Damascus.
90 CE	The composition of Luke's Gospel, in Antioch.
93 CE	Josephus publishes his *Antiquities of the Jews*.
95 CE	The Epistle to the Hebrews.
100 CE	The composition of John's Gospel, in Ephesus.
111 CE	Letter from the Emperor Trajan to Pliny, the governor of Bithynia and Pontus.
177 CE	Executions of Christians in Lyons during the reign of Marcus Aurelius.
313 CE	Constantine and Licinius agree the Edict of Milan.
325 CE	The Council of Nicea resolves a common creed.
367 CE	Festal letter of Athanasius.
451 CE	The Creed of Chalcedon.

CHAPTER 3: BASICS IN THE MIDDLE AGES

410 CE	The sack of Rome under Alaric.
525 CE	Chronology of Dionysius Exiguus.
627 CE	Defeat of the Sassanid Persians by Heraclius.
636 CE	Muslim victory at Yarmuk.
800 CE	Charlemagne anointed "Emperor of the Romans."
1095	Urban II's declaration of the First Crusade.
1146	Peter the Venerable claims that God rejects "the Jews like the hateful Cain, the Muslims like the worshippers of Baal."

1939–45	The Second World War.
1948	Founding of the State of Israel and of the World Council of Churches
1962	Opening of the Second Vatican Council
1963	Martin Luther King, Jr.'s letter from Birmingham jail, "The Negro is Your Brother."

THE BASICS OF JESUS
THE ORIGINS OF CHRISTIANITY IN THE FIRST CENTURY

When Jesus was born, probably in 2 CE, the Temple in Jerusalem constituted the ritual center of Judaism. Jews came from all over the known world to offer sacrifice according to the Torah, the Law of Moses as written in the first five books of the Scriptures of Israel.

THE COMMONLY ACCEPTED SYSTEM OF DATING

In 525 CE, a monk and scholar named Dionysius Exiguus established an historical chronology, taking Jesus' birth as the first "Year of the Lord" (*Anno Domini*, or "AD"). The system is still in use, with "BC" ("Before Christ") marking time prior to Jesus' birth. Today scholars commonly refer to dates as either "Before the Common Era" (BCE) or "Common Era" (CE). In setting out dates for events, Dionysius had to synchronize calendars from various regional governors and kingdoms, each with its own reckoning of dates. There had been no coordinated timeline, but schemes that followed the years of one reign or another, with differing views of when a new year even began. The timing he assigned has therefore been subject to correction as further data has been brought to bear and organized.

Herod the Great, who ruled as the client-king of Rome, had physically expanded the Temple, which stood on a stone plinth of some thirty-five acres that is still extant. The Herodian edifice is known as the Second Temple, since the First Temple, built by Solomon, had been destroyed in 586 BCE. The largest structure of its kind at the time, the Second Temple needed to be huge to accommodate the offerings of all Israel. According to the Torah only that one place on earth was acceptable to the God of Israel for the purpose of sacrifice.

Alongside this clear ritual center, the Torah guided the ethical behavior of Israelites. The Torah concerns not only basic moral instruction, but also commandments in regard to what foods should be eaten and other rules of purity. Sacrifice demanded that Israelites and their offerings be in a pure condition as they approached the God of Israel.

In addition to the written Torah, a group called the Pharisees held that *oral* Torah, teachings that they committed to memory, also needed to be followed. The oral Torah derived from Moses alongside the Scriptures in their view, but could only be accessed through the teachings of the Pharisees themselves. Because they held to additional regulations as necessary to make an Israelite pure, they came to be called "Separatists," the probable meaning of the term "Pharisee" in Hebrew. Inside the Temple itself, however, control of proceedings was in the hands of an hereditary priesthood among privileged families, allegedly derived from a priest named Zadok (and hence called the Sadducees in the Greek Gospels). They adhered to the written Torah alone.

TORAH OR LAW

Torah means "guidance" in Hebrew and refers to the revelation given to Moses in the period between the exodus and Israelite settlement in the land of Canaan. Rendered "law" (*nomos*) in Greek, the Torah addressed common behavior, the regulation of sacrifice, and the maintenance of that standard of purity that was expected of Israel as a sacrificial community. Alongside the written Torah (the biblical books called Genesis, Exodus, Leviticus, Numbers, and Deuteronomy), the Pharisees held that their oral traditions also reached back to Moses. Eventually, these oral traditions were written down also, in the work called the Mishnah (c. 200 CE).

As long as the Second Temple stood, Judaism during the first century adhered to the view that correct sacrifice there, together with adherence to the Law, would bring about the fulfillment of the promise to Abraham, the forefather of all Israel. Once settled in the Promised Land, God had assured Abraham that "all the families of the earth" would find their blessing in the Israelites (Genesis 12:3). This prophecy of future, virtually limitless expansion—an Israelite kingdom greater than any power on earth, reaching from the Nile to the Euphrates (Genesis 15:18)—fills out the religious system of Judaism during the Second Temple period. A clear goal and meaning animated a system of precise ritual and ethical commitment.

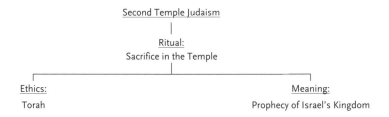

As a religious system, Judaism of this Second Temple period allowed great diversity in culture and yet unified Jews, most of whom by this time lived in what is called the Diaspora. Although the word literally means "dispersion" in Greek, by the first century Israelites occupied a vital and proud place among the civilized peoples from Babylon to Spain. Over the previous centuries Jewish emigration had been largely voluntary, although policies of deportation also played their part. For all the differences among Jews scattered around the Mediterranean world—in language, local custom, and even how to define Scripture—the ritual of the Temple, the Torah of Moses, and the promise of the Prophets gave them a common identity.

JESUS' FIRST REVOLUTION

Jesus was a revolutionary, but not because he headed up an insurrection. Nor did he set out deliberately to found a new religion. Yet the way he put the Judaism of his time into practice changed the religious system. That alteration affected the whole, and within only a few decades, a different religion emerged. All his basics were Jewish, but by means of two revolutions, Jesus arranged them into a new system.

One of the earliest sources within the Gospels is called "Q," an abbreviation of the German word *Quelle*, which means "source." Jesus' teaching was arranged in the form of a mishnah (a compilation of a rabbi's teaching by his disciples). This mishnah was preserved orally in Aramaic, Jesus' original language, and in a classic passage (Luke 10:1–12) it explained how his followers should act on his behalf. He sends them out as his personal representatives. The term used for "agent" in Greek (*apostolos*) comes into English as "apostle," the highest human authority, Jesus' envoy. As he delegates his followers, he explains his goals in the clearest possible way. Jesus' commission to them reflects the program of activity he embraced for himself and expected the apostles to follow.

Jesus instructs these disciples to travel without provisions. That seems strange, unless the image of the harvest at the beginning of the charge (Luke 10:2) is taken seriously. Because they are going out as to rich fields, they do not require what would normally be needed on a journey: purse, bag, and even sandals are all dispensed with (Luke 10:4). They should treat Israel as a field in which one works, not as an itinerary of travel. The support they receive as they make their way around Israel will be the sign whether their message is accepted or not.

Another powerful comparison is at work within this commission alongside its image of Israel as a land ready for harvest. Pilgrims who entered the Temple in Jerusalem also did so without the bags and staffs and purses that they had traveled with. All such items were to be deposited before worship, so that one was present without encumbrance, just as an Israelite. Part of worship was that one was to appear in one's simple purity, and that imperative was incorporated into the apostles' work.

By his program of constant travel within Israel, Jesus treated the whole of the land as holy, and he instructed his disciples to do the same—dispensing with the equipment of travel. He accepted hospitality in every place that he entered and even acquired the reputation of a "glutton and a drunkard," "a friend of sinners" (see Matthew 11:19 and Luke 7:34). For him any person who joined in eating with other Israelites, both forgiving and being forgiven for that purpose and acknowledging that God was the true host of the occasion, belonged in his fellowship. The apostles define and create the true Israel to which they are sent, and they tread that territory as on holy ground, shoeless and without staff or purse.

The meaning behind this activity on behalf of extending purity into Israel is grounded in Jesus' characteristic prayer, known as the Lord's Prayer or the Paternoster. The New Testament includes two versions of the Lord's Prayer (Matthew 6:9–13; Luke 11:2–4), both of which derive from the source known as "Q." Luke's is widely considered the earlier in form, and it does seem plain that Matthew presents what is, in effect, a commentary woven together with the prayer. The relative sparseness of Luke has won it recognition among scholars as the nearest to the form of an outline which Jesus recommended to his followers.

Matthew	Luke

Our father,
    who is in the heavens,
your name will be sanctified,
your kingdom will come,
    your will happen
    as in heaven, even on earth.
Our bread that is coming,
    give us today,
and release us our debts,
    as we also have released our debtors,
	Father,
	
	your name will be sanctified,
	your kingdom will come.
	
	Our bread that is coming,
	be giving us each day,
	and release us our sins,
	    because we also ourselves
	    release everyone who is
	    indebted us,

And do not bring us to the test, but deliver us from the evil one.	And do not bring us to the test.

One Gospel cannot be explained on the basis of literal copying from another Gospel. Matthew reflects the use of the prayer in a congregation of believers, while Luke is geared more for private use. In the renderings of the Greek texts above, indented material is widely considered to be commentary that helped explain the prayer.

A model is at issue in Jesus' teaching, rather than a precise repetition of words. (Jesus warned against mechanical or wordy prayer, Matthew 6:7.) The basic model of the Lord's Prayer consists of calling God father, rejoicing that his name shall be sanctified and that his kingdom shall come, and then asking for daily bread, forgiveness, and not to be brought to the test.

The model unfolds under two major headings:

I) an address of God (1) as father, (2) with sanctification of God's name, and (3) vigorous assent to the coming of God's kingdom;
II) a petition for (1) bread, (2) forgiveness, and (3) constancy.

Assessed by its individual elements, the Lord's Prayer may be characterized as a fairly typical instance of Judaic practice in its period. In particular, Jesus reflects the oral, memorized culture of Jewish Galilee, where the Psalms were known by heart and used in the course of worship. To call God "father" was—in itself—not unusual. Psalm 103:13 associates God's fatherly care with his actual provision for prayerful Israel: "As a father has compassion upon his children, so does the LORD have compassion upon those who fear him."

The same Psalm (103:1) shows that the connection of God's "holy name" to his fatherhood was seen as natural. Sanctifying God's name acknowledges that holiness, and the earliest of Rabbinic texts of prayer—such as the Kaddish, which means "Sanctified [be God's name]"—insist on that recognition. That God's holiness is consistent with people being forgiven and accepted by him is the foundational motif of Psalm 103, where the singer calls on his own soul to bless the LORD "who pardons all you iniquities and heals all your diseases" (Psalm 103:3). Finally, this psalm portrays God as the hand that guides creation and revelation, so in nature as well as in the justice that emerges in human society, "his Kingdom rules over all" (Psalm 103:19).

The initial point of Jesus' model of prayer is that God is to be approached as father, his name sanctified, and his Kingdom welcomed. The act of prayer along those lines, with great variety over time and from place to place and tradition to tradition, has been a hallmark of Christianity.

To address God as one's father, and then to sanctify his name, acknowledges ambivalence in the human attitude toward God. He approaches us freely and without restraint, and yet is unapproachable, as holy as we are ordinary. The welcoming of his Kingdom, of his comprehensive rule of justice within the moral ambiguities of this world, wills away this ambivalence. God's intimate holiness is to invade the ordinary, so that any sense of estrangement is overcome.

The three elements which open the prayer characterize a relationship and an attitude toward God which the one who prays makes his own or her own. The distinctiveness of the prayer is nothing other than that consciousness of God that Jesus enjoyed. Awareness of God and of oneself is what Christians kindle when they pray the Lord's Prayer. And at the same time, the prayer is nothing other than the Lord's; whatever the power of such a consciousness, it is only ours because it was Christ's first. That is why the consciousness of praying in this manner produces relationship: one is God's child and Jesus' sister or brother in the same instant.

In this case, as in others, a basic of Christianity first emerged in Aramaic, the language of Jesus and his earliest followers. A Semitic tongue similar to Hebrew, it is nonetheless a different language; that is why the Hebrew Bible had to be translated into Aramaic during the time of Jesus. (The result is called *targum*, a term that means "translation" in Aramaic.) But the Gospels and all the other books in the New Testament were composed in Greek. They are based in a large proportion upon Aramaic sources, but their writing is firmly located in the "common" Greek dialect (the *Koine*) of the first century. Yet the elements of the Lord's Prayer are clearly drawn from the Judaic tradition, and Aramaic wording can be identified as the source of the Greek texts of Matthew and Luke:

'abba	father/source
yitqadash shemakh	your name will be sanctified
tetey malkhutakh	your kingdom will come
hav li yoma lakhma d'ateh	give me today the bread that is coming
ushebaq li yat chobati	and release me my debts
ve'al ta'eleyni lenisyona	not bring me to the test

Although the individual parts of the whole are common, Jesus assembled them in a way that produced a shift in the religious system of Judaism. Prophecy of the coming Kingdom had been the meaning behind both ritual and ethics, but in Jesus' practice,

the true meaning of all human activity—and the opening
of the prayer—was instead the relationship to God as Father.
That becomes forever the determinative focus among the disciples of
Jesus.

The Kingdom remains vital, but in a new way. Instead of
its being the aim and meaning of ritual and ethics, Jesus prays for
the prophetic Kingdom *within human experience*, as Matthew
explains it, "on earth as in heaven." Prophecy of God's Kingdom,
rather than the Kingdom of Israel, is now a principle of ethics, of
people acting in such a way that God is known as Father. That is
why Jesus tells parables of God as a King that also convey how he
wants his followers to behave. They should be as welcoming of the
poor as the king who opened his son's wedding feast to the indi-
gent (Matthew 22:1–10) and as forgiving as the king who decided
that he would cancel the enormous debts he was owed (Matthew
18:23–35).

The parables of Jesus are not just pictures of how God acts; they
are also models of how God's children are to act. Jesus displaced the
Torah as the ground of ethics, because for him the Kingdom
defined how to behave: the Kingdom realizes in action what it
means to acknowledge the human connection to God. Prophecy
that the Kingdom will grow from the seed of hope to the full
enjoyment of God's presence with his children (Mark 4:26–29),
rather than the Law as given to Moses, becomes the controlling
authority in Christian ethics. That was Jesus' first revolution, and he
gave his program ritual expression in his practice of meals before
the Last Supper.

SACRED MEALS PRIOR TO THE EUCHARIST

Meals in Judaism were regular expressions of social solidarity
and of common identity as Israel, the people of God. Many
sorts of meals are attested in the literature of early Judaism.
From Qumran we learn of banquets at which the community convened in order of hierarchy; the Pharisees shared
meals within fellowships at which like-minded colleagues
would share the foods and the company they considered
pure. Ordinary households might welcome the coming of the

Sabbath with a prayer of sanctification over a cup of wine, or open a family occasion with a blessing over bread and wine.

Jesus' meals in Galilee, long before his Last Supper, were similar in some ways to several of these meals, but they were also distinctive. He had a characteristic understanding of what the meals meant and of who should participate in them. For him, eating socially with others in Israel was a parable of the feast in the kingdom that was to come. The idea that God would offer festivity for all peoples on his holy mountain (see Isaiah 2:2–4) was a key feature in the fervent expectations of Judaism during the first century, and Jesus shared that hope from an early stage, as can be seen in a saying from the source called "Q" (see Matthew 8:11 = Luke 13:28, 29): "Many shall come from east and west, and feast with Abraham, Isaac, and Jacob in the kingdom of God."

Jesus represented a prophetic form of the religion of his time that was often not in phase with the insistence on stability that characterized establishment figures in the Temple. He emphasized the ethical demands of God's Kingdom *and* identified God's Fatherhood, rather than the prophecy of Israel's Kingdom, as the central meaning that made sense of ritual and ethics alike.

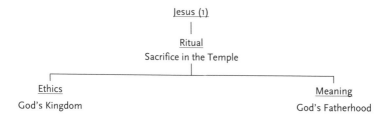

Jesus (1)
|
Ritual
Sacrifice in the Temple
|
Ethics   Meaning
God's Kingdom   God's Fatherhood

The Gospels most clearly represent Jesus' change in the system of Judaism by means of his teaching on how the purpose of the Torah is fulfilled, not by performing its laws, but by realizing the relationships of love that God desires. The most direct expression of Jesus' principle concerning love appears in Matthew and Mark (Matthew 22:34–40; Mark 12:28–34):

The Pharisees heard that he had shut the Zadokites up, and were gathered together in the same place. And one from them, a lawyer, interrogated him, testing him: Teacher, which decree is great in the law? But he told him, You shall love the Lord your God with all your heart and with all your life and with all your mind: the great and first decree is this. A second is like it: You shall love your neighbor as yourself. On these two decrees all the Law is suspended–and the Prophets!

One of the scribes came forward– hearing them arguing (seeing that he answered them well)–and interrogated him, Which is the first decree of all? Jesus answered that: First is, Hear, Israel, our God is the Lord; he is one Lord. And you shall love the Lord your God from all your heart and from all your life and from all your mind and from all your strength. This is second: You shall love your neighbor as yourself. There is not another decree greater than these. And the scribe said to him, Fine, teacher: in truth you have said that he is one and there is not another beside him, and to love him from all heart and from all the understanding and from all the strength and to love the neighbor as oneself is overflowing all burnt offerings and sacrifices. Jesus saw he answered sensibly and answered, said to him: You are not far from the kingdom of God. And no one any longer dared to interrogate him.

In both Gospels, Jesus is asked by someone outside his group—a Pharisee in Matthew, a scribe in Mark—what is the great (Matthew) or first (Mark) commandment. He replies by citing two commandments from the Torah, to love God (drawing from Deuteronomy 6:4, 5) and love one's neighbor (drawing from a different biblical book, Leviticus 19:18).

Jesus concludes in Matthew that all the Law (the Torah) and the Prophets of the Bible hang from those two commandments, while in Mark he says more simply that there is no other commandment greater than these. Jesus seized upon imperatives from different parts of the Torah in order to discover the grounding message of the Bible.

Matthew and Mark make sense of Jesus' teaching differently, as is only natural, since they were written a generation after the time of Jesus, and each Gospel addresses its own situation in life. In Matthew, the organic connection among the commandments assures that they all hang together (with the teaching of the Prophets) on the principle of love toward God and neighbor (Matthew 22:40). Mark, on the other hand, has the scribe who initiated the scene conclude that to love is more than all burnt offerings and sacrifices (Mark 12:32–33).

The interpretation of Jesus' teaching in Matthew moves in the direction of claiming that Jesus represents the fulfillment of the Law and the Prophets, a thematic concern of this Gospel generally. The interpretation of Jesus' teaching in Mark takes the tack that Jesus' principle establishes a non-ritual means of approval by God, a concern typical of Mark.

Both Matthew and Mark find their center of gravity, however, in the conviction that the commandment to love God and love one's neighbor is the action that unites one with Jesus in an approach to God. The emblem of that approach is fulfillment of the Law and the Prophets in Matthew (22:40), nearness to the Kingdom of God in Mark (12:34). The differences between those interpretations are not to be minimized: they represent the substantive independence of the Gospels as methods of teaching new believers. But the agreement between Matthew and Mark that love is the means of access to God after the pattern of Jesus is an equally striking attribute. The synthesis of the two imperatives, to love God and to love one's neighbor, into a single principle is Jesus' contribution, a permanent part of Christianity's inheritance.

The Jewish teacher Hillel, a near contemporary of Jesus, is said to have taught—in a dictum comparable to Jesus' teaching—that the Torah is a commentary on the injunction not to do what is hateful to one's neighbor (Shabbath 31a in the Babylonian Talmud). The centrality of the commandment to love one's neighbor is also asserted by Aqiba, the famous rabbi of the second century (in the midrash or interpretation of Leviticus called Sifra, Leviticus 19:18). Differences of emphasis are detectable and important, but the fact remains that Jesus does not appear to have been exceptional in locating love at the center of the divine commandments. Any rabbi, a teacher in a city or a local village, might have come up with some such principle, although the expressions of the principle attributed to Jesus are especially apt.

Precisely because Jesus' teaching has clear precedents in the early Judaism of his day in terms of content, it becomes clear that the tradition presented in aggregate by Matthew and Mark highlights Jesus' originality in explaining the nature of the love he demanded of his followers. Jesus' citation of the two biblical passages that demand and define love is for both Matthew and Mark no longer simply a matter of locating a coherent principle within the Torah, in answer to the literal challenge of the question of the Pharisee or scribe. Rather, the twin commandment of love is now held to be a transcendent principle, which fulfills (so Matthew) or supersedes (so Mark) the Torah. Christ himself, by citing and enacting that principle, is held to offer the ethical key to communion with God.

Luke's version of the teaching concerning love is quite different from what we find in Matthew and Mark, and yet comes by a different route to the same basic message. Luke makes it especially apparent that the significance of Jesus' message lies at least as much in who Jesus is when he speaks as in what he says (Luke 10:25–37):

> And look, there arose some lawyer, testing him out, saying, Teacher, having done what shall I inherit perpetual life? But he said to him, In the Law what is written—how do you read it? He answered and said, You shall love the Lord your God from all your heart and with all your life and with all your strength and with all your mind, and your neighbor as yourself. Yet he said to him, You answered rightly: do this, and you will live. He wanted to justify himself and said to Jesus, And who is my neighbor? Jesus took up, and said, Some person went down from Jerusalem to Jericho, and thugs fell upon him, who stripped him and inflicted lesions. They went away, leaving him half-dead. But by coincidence some priest went down that way; he saw him and passed by opposite. Likewise also a Levite came by the place, but he saw and passed by opposite. Some Samaritan made a way and came by him, saw and felt for him. He came forward and, pouring on oil and wine, wrapped his wounds. He mounted him up on his own animal and led him to a hostel and took care of him. On the next day he put out two denarii and gave them to the hosteller and said, Take care of him, and that: Should you spend over, I will repay you when I come back again. Of these three, who seems to you to have become neighbor to the one who fell among the thugs? Yet he said, The one who did mercy with him. But Jesus said to him, Proceed: and you do likewise.

Here an unidentified "lawyer," rather than the Pharisee of Matthew or the scribe of Mark, asks what to do in order to inherit eternal life. In fact, it is not Jesus in Luke who cites the twin principles of love, but the lawyer himself (10:27).

At first, Jesus merely confirms what the lawyer already knows (10:28). Jesus' peculiar contribution comes in the response to the lawyer's further question, Who is my neighbor (10:29)? The question and the response appear in material found only in Luke (10:29–37), the presentation of Jesus' teaching concerning love that was characteristic of the church in Antioch (around the year 90 CE) where the Gospel according to Luke seems to have been composed.

Luke's expression of the principle of love, in distinction from Matthew's and Mark's, explicitly makes Jesus' *application* of the commandment, rather than its formulation, his systemic innovation. The innovation is effected in the parable of the Good Samaritan (Luke 10:29–37). Whether Jesus himself told the parable in just the way Luke presents is beside the present point. What concerns us is that (1) the parable informs the commandment to love with a new emphasis, and that (2) the new emphasis is the center of Luke's ethics, as distinct from Matthew's or Mark's ethics.

Literally, the parable is designed to answer the question, Who is my neighbor? And that formal issue is also addressed at the close of the parable, when Jesus tells his questioner to go and do what the Samaritan did, that is: show himself a neighbor to one in obvious need (10:37). But the literal issue in this case is distinct from the underlying issue.

The underlying challenge is not the goodness of the Samaritan, but the fact that he *is* a Samaritan. The victim of the mugging is in no position to complain in his wounded condition, but especially as a recent pilgrim to Jerusalem, any Jew not in mortal danger might well have objected to contact with a Samaritan.

Samaritan sacrifice on Mount Gerizim was antagonistic to Judaic sacrifice in the Temple on Mount Zion. The Samaritan practice derived from the tenth century BCE, when the northern part of Israel rebelled against the Davidic monarchy and seceded to form a separate state. From the point of view of Judaism, the Samaritans were apostate not only because they rebelled against the house of David, but also because their sacrifices on Mount Gerizim included practices from surrounding cultures that violated the Law of Moses.

A priest and a Levite have already passed by in Jesus' parable. The wounded man might have been dead, and the Torah's teaching prevented contact with corpses by those involved in serving the Temple (Leviticus 21:1–4). In the parable, then, a victim who *seemed* impure is aided by a Samaritan who *definitely was* impure.

Nonetheless, Jesus says that the Samaritan's action fulfills the commandment to love one's neighbor as oneself.

The parable of the good Samaritan is a story that formally conveys how to be a neighbor and also how to identify a neighbor. It is shaped to insist that one viewed as "impure" may be a neighbor to one who is "pure." The commandment to love is such that, in its application, it creates a new sphere of purity that transcends any other notion of what is clean and what is unclean.

Jesus' first revolution reached many sympathetic hearers and followers in Galilee. Taken in its own terms, the success of the message up until this point was enough to make the local ruler want to eliminate Jesus as a prophetic rabbi who might mount a political challenge (Luke 13:31–33). Against the view of the Temple leadership, he did not see the Torah as the ultimate measure of ethics. Rather, God provided that measure by the way his Kingdom was revealed among those who related to him as their Father. But the appeal of Jesus at this stage was understood within Judaism, although in its prophetic form rather than along the lines of the Temple establishment. The full extent of his change in the religious system was not immediately obvious. The arc of his development, and the emergence of the religion he founded, only came into plain view at the stage of his second revolution.

JESUS' SECOND REVOLUTION

A skilled oral teacher, Jesus was called a "rabbi," a title applied to him in the Gospels more than others (including "Son of God" and "Christ"). He wove a portrait of God as a divine ruler (of his "Kingdom") together with an appeal to people to behave as God's children (by loving their divine father and their neighbor). Referring to himself as God's "Son," he expected his followers to treat God as their father and also to become God's sons.

Yet Jesus posed a threat to Jewish and Roman authorities in Jerusalem. He would not have been crucified otherwise. A basic question emerges out of the relationship between Jesus the rabbi and Jesus the criminal: What brought a teacher of God's ways and God's love to the deliberately cruel death of Roman crucifixion?

The Gospels answer that question when they all relate an incident (Matthew 21:12–16; Mark 11:15–18; Luke 19:45–48; John 2:14–22) traditionally called "The Cleansing of the Temple." Jesus boldly enters the holy place where sacrifice was conducted and *throws out* both those who sold offerings and moneychangers who were converting the currency of Rome into money that was acceptable to the priestly authorities. Jesus' action threatened the priests because an important source of revenue was jeopardized. Roman interests were engaged because Pontius Pilate, the local magistrate, needed to keep order in the Temple, one of the most important sites of worship in the empire.

Jesus' act in the Temple was not, as is sometimes supposed, a general objection to sacrifice. He took the practice of sacrifice for granted; that was the point of the Temple where he worshipped many times. Rather, he occupied the Temple with his followers to prevent the purchase of animals in the holy place. That trade involved commerce within the Temple, and the Jesus of the canonical Gospels, like the Jesus of the *Gospel according to Thomas*, held that "Traders and merchants shall not enter the places of my father" (*Thomas*, saying 64).

The purpose of Jesus' occupation makes good sense in the context of what we know of the activities of other early rabbinic teachers. Hillel was an older contemporary of Jesus', who, as we have seen, taught a form of ethics comparable to Jesus'. He also taught about worship in the Temple in a way that can be compared to Jesus' approach (in the Babylonian Talmud; see Bavli tractate Besa 20a, b). Hillel insisted that, when the people of Israel came to worship, they should offer of their own property, putting their hands on the animal that was about to be sacrificed as a statement of ownership.

Jesus' occupation of the Temple is best seen as an attempt like Hillel's to insist that the offerer's actual ownership of what is offered forms a vital aspect of sacrifice. This was also the principle of the prophet Zechariah (see Zechariah 14:16–21), who prophesied that even the Gentiles would one day offer sacrifice in Jerusalem— without the demand of any payment and without any middlemen whatsoever. But when Jesus came to the Temple at the end of his life, he saw that the high priest Caiaphas had introduced the traders into the Temple. Caiaphas removed them from their usual location across the valley from the Temple and brought them into the holy courtyard that surrounded the altar complex.

From the point of view of efficiency, Caiaphas' innovation was sensible. One could know at the moment of purchase that one's sacrifice was acceptable and not run the risk of harm befalling the animal on its way to be slaughtered. But when we look at the installation of the traders from the point of view of Hillel's teaching, Jesus' objection becomes understandable. Not only did Caiaphas introduce the necessity for commerce into the Temple, betraying the prophecy of Zechariah; he also broke the link between the worshiper's ownership and offering within the ritual action.

Jesus called Caiaphas and his cohort a bunch of thieves, quoting Jeremiah 7:11, and implicitly invoking Jeremiah's prophecy of the Temple's destruction (see Matthew 21:13; Mark 11:17; Luke 19:46). But the implication was only that, and Caiaphas exaggerated the threat Jesus posed to turn the Romans against him. Once the Gospels were written, their increasingly non-Jewish readers conceived of Jesus as opposing the whole system of sacrifice. But the force of Jesus' original message concerned what the Temple should be, rather than its demolition.

Jesus' interference in the ordinary worship of the Temple could by itself have brought about his execution. The Temple was the center of Judaism for as long as it stood. Roman officials were so interested in its smooth functioning at the hands of the priests they appointed that they were known to sanction the penalty of death for serious sacrilege. Emperors even paid for sacrifices to be offered in the Temple, so that its smooth operation served Roman hegemony as well as Israel's worship. Yet there is no indication that Jesus was arrested immediately after his intervention in the Temple.

Instead, he remained free for some time and was finally taken into custody just after one of his meals, the Last Supper (Matthew 26:47–56; Mark 14:43–52; Luke 22:47–53; John 18:3–11). The decision of the authorities of the Temple to move against Jesus when they did is what made it Jesus' final supper.

Why did the authorities wait and why did they act when they did? The Gospels portray them as fearful of the popular backing that Jesus enjoyed (Matthew 26:5; Mark 14:2; Luke 22:2; John 11:47–48), and he did bring zealous followers into the Temple with him. But, in addition, there was another factor: Jesus could not simply be dispatched as a cultic criminal. He was not attempting an onslaught upon the Temple as such; his dispute with the authorities concerned the right way to sacrifice within the Temple.

The delay of the Jewish authorities, then, was understandable. It was also commendable, reflecting continued controversy over the merits of Jesus' teaching and whether his occupation should be condemned out of hand. Why did they finally arrest Jesus? The Last Supper provides the key; something about Jesus' meals after his occupation of the Temple caused Judas to inform on Jesus. Of course, "Judas" is the only name that the traditions of the New Testament have left us. We cannot say who or how many of the disciples became disaffected by Jesus' behavior after his occupation of the Temple.

THE LAST SUPPER

The authorities in Jerusalem arrested Jesus just after the supper we call "Last." He continued to celebrate fellowship at table as a foretaste of the kingdom, just as he had before. But he also added a new and scandalous dimension of meaning after his occupation of the Temple. Jesus said of the wine, "This is my blood," and of the bread, "This is my flesh" (Matthew 26:26, 28 = Mark 14:22, 24 = Luke 22:19–20 = 1 Corinthians 11:24–25). In Jesus' context, the context of his confrontation with the authorities of the Temple, his words can have had only one meaning. He cannot have meant, "Here are my personal body and blood;" that is an interpretation which only makes sense at a later stage (introduced in the last Gospel in the New Testament, John 6:53–56). Jesus' point was rather that, since the Temple was defiled by priestly dominance, wine was his blood of sacrifice and bread was his flesh of sacrifice. In his own context, Jesus was saying that his meals were more acceptable to his Father than sacrifice in the Temple, and that was the basis of the charge of blasphemy against him.

After they learned of Jesus' new interpretation of his meals of fellowship, the authorities arrested him. From his early days in Galilee, Jesus had celebrated fellowship at table as a foretaste of the

Kingdom. And in the Last Supper, as well, the promise of drinking new wine in the Kingdom of God joined his followers in an anticipatory celebration of the Kingdom (Matthew 26:29; Mark 14:25; Luke 22:18). That is why this meal, in Christian tradition variously called the Lord's Supper, Eucharist, and Mass, is consistently spoken of as "celebrated." Even though inevitably associated with Jesus' death, it rejoices in the promise of the Kingdom.

EUCHARIST

The emblematic communal ritual of Christianity is most widely known as the Eucharist, from the Greek word that means "thanksgiving" (*eukharistia*). That term was used because the purpose of the meal was, from its origin, to thank God for the arrival of his Kingdom. Because of its close association with Jesus, the meal was also known as the Lord's Supper and Communion within the New Testament. From the final words of the Latin celebration of the ritual, it later became known as the Mass.

The meaning of the Last Supper evolved over a series of meals after Jesus' occupation of the Temple. During that period, Jesus claimed that wine and bread were a better sacrifice than what was offered in the Temple, a foretaste of new wine in the Kingdom of God. At least wine and bread were Israel's own, not tokens of priestly dominance. Opposition to him, even among the twelve (in the shape of Judas, according to the Gospels) became deadly. In essence, Jesus made his meals into a rival altar.

Jesus' new meal gave Caiaphas what he needed. Jesus could be charged with blasphemy: the issue now was not simply Jesus' objection to commercial arrangements, but his creation of an alternative sacrifice outside the Temple. He blasphemed the Law of Moses, and Rome's interests also came into play. The Temple in Jerusalem had come to symbolize Roman power, as well as the devotion of Israel. Rome guarded jealously the sacrifices that the emperor financed in Jerusalem, so that prayer was offered on his behalf. (When that gift was refused in 66 CE, the refusal was understood in Rome as a declaration of war.) Jesus stood accused of creating a disturbance in that Temple during his occupation and of fomenting disloyalty to it and therefore to Caesar. His execution became inevitable.

JESUS' RESURRECTION

Modern Judaism is unlike its ancient counterpart in some ways. Today many Jews see an interest in the afterlife as a Christian preserve. But during the first century CE, most Jews believed that the righteous would awake from death to what the book of Daniel calls "eternal life" (Daniel 12:2–3). How and when resurrection occurs have always been a matter for debate and discussion, but ancient Judaism cannot be understood apart from the belief that God vindicates just people. Jesus' disciples believed that he had been vindicated by resurrection, much as the prophet Elijah had been taken up to heaven alive (2 Kings 2:1–15).

It is no coincidence that the typical setting of appearances of the risen Jesus is while disciples were taking meals together. The conviction that the light of God's Kingdom radiated from that practice went hand in hand with the conviction that the true master of the table, the rabbi who began the practice, remained among his followers.

THE EUCHARIST IN THE CIRCLE OF PETER

The "blessing" or breaking of bread at home, the *berakhah* of Judaism, became a principal model of the Eucharist in the practice of the disciples who gathered around Peter after Jesus' resurrection. A practical result of that development was that bread came to have precedence over wine. This reversed Jesus' habit in Galilee and Jerusalem, when he followed the pattern of the meal called a *Kiddush* (sanctification), which welcomed in the sacred time of the Sabbath or another feast of Judaism. The circle of Peter conceived of Jesus risen from the dead as a new Moses, who gave commands as Moses did on Sinai and who also expected his followers to worship on Mount Zion. Peter's adherents congregated in the homes of their colleagues, rather than seeking the hospitality of others, and they practiced sacrifice in the Temple (see Acts 2:43–47). They adapted the celebration of the Eucharist to the household blessing of bread in their domestic meals.

The experience of Jesus after he was raised from the dead must have varied widely, because his resurrected presence is described in very different ways in the New Testament. But whatever the description, he was understood as what Paul calls a "spiritual body" (1 Corinthians 15:44): "body," because the presence was recognizable as Jesus, but "spiritual," because he was not present as ordinary flesh, but in enduring Spirit.

The disciples' belief that the risen Jesus encountered them with God's Spirit and that they shared that Spirit with him caused them to communicate their experience to others. The finale of Matthew's Gospel portrays Jesus as telling his followers to "make disciples of all nations, baptizing them in the name of the Father, and of the Son, and of the Holy Spirit" (Matthew 28:19). This scene, like the more famous scene of Pentecost in the Book of Acts (Acts 2:1–41), marks another pivotal change in the development of Judaism into Christianity.

At Pentecost, the summer feast of harvest, the Spirit is portrayed as descending on the twelve apostles (including Matthias, to replace Judas). They speak God's praises in the various languages of those assembled from the four points of the compass, both Jews and proselytes (Acts 2:1–12). The mention of proselytes (2:11) and the specification that those gathered came from "every nation under heaven" (2:5) clearly point ahead to the inclusion of non-Jews by means of baptism within Acts. Even Peter's explanation of the descent of the Spirit underlines that. He quotes from the prophet Joel (3:1–5 in the Septuagint; Acts 2:17–21): "And it will be in the last days, says God, that I will pour out from my spirit upon all flesh." "All flesh," not only historic Israel, is to receive God's Spirit.

PENTECOST

Seven weeks after the close of the entire festival of Passover and Unleavened Bread came the feast called Weeks or

Pentecost (in Greek, referring to the period of fifty days that was involved; see Leviticus 23:15–22; Deuteronomy 16:9–12). The waving of the barley sheaf before the LORD at the close of Passover anticipated the greater harvest of wheat which was to follow, and that is just what Weeks celebrates (so Leviticus 23:10–15). The timing of the coming of the Holy Spirit in the recollection of Peter's circle is unequivocal (Acts 2:1–4), and the theme of Moses dispensing of the Spirit on his elders is reflected (see Numbers 11:11–29). The feast of Weeks could be associated with Noah's covenant (see the noncanonical but ancient text found among the Dead Sea Scrolls, *Jubilees* 6:1, 10–11, 17–19). Because Noah was the ancestor of all human beings, not only Israelites, the Pentecost connection may help to explain why the coming of the Spirit then was to extend to humanity at large (see Acts 2:5–11).

The Spirit that is poured out, in the experience of Jesus' followers, comes directly from the majesty of God, from his rule over creation as a whole. This is the same Spirit that hovered over the waters at the beginning of creation (Genesis 1:1), rather than anything limited to Israel. Jesus once claimed that he proclaimed God's kingdom on the authority of God's Spirit (Matthew 12:28). Now, as a consequence of the resurrection, Jesus had poured out that same Spirit upon those who would follow him. Baptism in the Spirit (see Acts 1:4–5) and baptism into the name of Jesus were for apostolic Christianity one and the same for that reason.

The Spirit, as released in baptism into the name of Jesus, distinguishes the practice of the Church from the practice of Judaism in regard to immersion in water. Jewish practitioners such as John the Baptist had called Israelites to "immerse" in water (which is just what the Greek term *baptizo* means), but this baptism was a repetitive ritual designed to remove impurity. Many forms of purification other than John's existed, because impurity was a fact of life, as routine as childbirth and preparing a loved one's body for burial, for example. Purification had to be repetitive. The contrast that the risen Jesus makes in Acts demonstrates the transformation of the immersion ritual (Acts 1:5): "John indeed baptized with water, while you will be baptized in Holy Spirit."

Baptism changes so profoundly after the resurrection that its whole medium alters. The medium in John's immersion was water, because the issue was purification; the medium of baptism into the name of Jesus is Spirit, because the issue is the empowerment that Spirit brings. As the risen Jesus goes on to say: "But you will receive power when the Holy Spirit has come upon you, and you will become my witnesses both in Jerusalem and all Judaea and Samaria, even to the end of the earth" (Acts 1:8). Because this Spirit is God's, it only needs to be given once, so that Christian baptism is a ritual that is not repeated, and it can be given to all people, not just to Israelites, because it is rooted in their creation by God, rather than in any ethnic identity whatever.

As a result of the resurrection of Jesus, therefore, baptism in a new definition joined the Eucharist as the emblematic ritual of the new movement. The immersion ritual made the claim of the intimacy of God's presence as father all the stronger to believers and gave them an enlivened personal sense of the possibilities of prophecy.

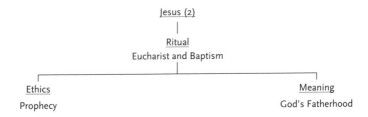

With these basics in place, Jesus' movement began to emerge as a religion distinct from Judaism, although it would take until the end of the first century for this to be evident to most observers. There is no critical doubt about Jesus' role as the most influential teacher in the religion, both in life and as raised from the dead, but only subsequent events would crystallize his movement into a new religion, rather than a branch within Judaism.

SUMMARY

In this chapter we have seen how Jesus changed Judaism:

- He identified God's Fatherhood as the primary meaning of the religious system.

- He portrayed his Prophecy of God's Kingdom, rather than the Torah, as the basis of ethical behavior.
- His distinctive practice brought him into conflict with the authorities in the Temple, and he opposed their commercial practice both by interfering with customary sacrifice and by making his meals with his disciples into a replacement of the altar.
- Even his death produced a radical change, because his disciples experienced God's Spirit coming to them as a result of Jesus' resurrection, so that they also had a prophetic role.
- Baptism emerged with the Eucharist as a means by which all peoples, not just Israelites, could inherit all the promises made to Israel.

FURTHER READING

Barrett, C. K. (1994) *The Acts of the Apostles* I: The International Critical Commentary (Edinburgh: Clark).

Chilton, Bruce (2000) *Rabbi Jesus. An Intimate Biography* (New York: Doubleday).

Chilton, Bruce (2010) *The Way of Jesus. To Repair and Renew the World* (Nashville, TN: Abingdon).

Hartman, Lars (1997) *"Into the Name of the Lord Jesus." Baptism in the Early Church:* Studies of the New Testament and its World (Edinburgh: Clark).

Meier, John P. (1991) *A Marginal Jew. Rethinking the Historical Jesus* (New York: Doubleday).

Skarsaune, Oskar (2002) *In the Shadow of the Temple. Jewish Influences on Early Christianity* (Downers Grove, IL: InterVarsity Press).

Snodgrass, Klyne R. (2008) *Stories with Intent. A Comprehensive Guide to the Parables of Jesus* (Grand Rapids, MI: Eerdmans).

CATHOLIC, ORTHODOX BASICS
CLASSIC FOUNDATIONS OF CHRISTIANITY

The last chapter explained how Jesus' followers reconceived ritual immersion in Judaism so as to symbolize baptism into the Spirit of God. They believed that their rabbi's resurrection signaled that God poured his Spirit on "all flesh," not just on the people of Israel; their conviction marked a major change in the movement. The outreach to Gentiles by the disciples after Jesus' death provoked the most profound shift ever seen in the history of Christian thought and practice, and forced the fledgling movement to confront a contentious issue.

As believers included Gentiles within a conception of a single, all-embracing Church, they made two characteristic claims about their fellowship. They asserted that their reach was "catholic," a term that means universal in geographical extent. Believers saw themselves as sharing identity with Christians throughout the Roman Empire. The faith that bound them together, they insisted, was "orthodox" or rightly thought. The terms "Catholic" and "Orthodox" were both used from an early stage to express the twin claims of universal reach and doctrinal truth. At a much later stage, during the Middle Ages, "Catholic" came to be applied to the Church in the West and "Orthodox" to the Church in the East. Originally, however, they were used together as an expression of unity that emerged out of the successful resolution of the controversy of how a single Church could include Jews and Gentiles together.

DEFINING WHO IS A CHRISTIAN

The book of Acts presents this shift as the result of the apostle Peter's prophetic experience and activity. The significance of his prophecy is underlined, because it is narrated three times (Acts 10, 11, and 15), a characteristic way for Acts to draw attention to the significance of an event.

In the first telling of the story (Acts 9:38–10:48) Peter sojourns among the coastal cities of Lydda, Joppa, and Caesarea, cities dominated by Hellenistic culture that served as centers of Roman military and commercial control. Famous as Jesus' disciple, Peter becomes known to Cornelius, a centurion. Roman office conferred wealth, privilege, and relative independence. Although a Gentile, Cornelius pursued his attraction to the God of Israel. Guided by prayer, he seeks out Peter.

ANGELS

Prayer in the New Testament, particularly in the book of Acts, frequently involves a divine response, as well as a person's address to God. God's answer might come in the form of a "messenger," or "angel" (from the Greek term *anggelos*, equivalent to the Hebrew *malakh*). Israelites conceived of God as reigning in his heavenly Kingdom, surrounded by angelic courtiers. He responded to prayer by dispatching an angel, and the messenger might be experienced visually, in audible words, or as interior illumination. Most of the texts involved focus more on the substance of the message from God than on the characteristics of the messenger, since the angel functions as a medium of the contact that prayer establishes.

An angel tells Cornelius, a Gentile searcher for the God of Israel known as a "God-fearer," to contact Peter. A vision also comes to Peter—and is repeated twice—instructing him to overcome his ritual and ethnic aversion to Gentiles. Messengers from Cornelius arrive with an invitation to Peter to accept hospitality in Cornelius' house—which would result in violating Jewish purity laws. Prompted by his vision, Peter accepts the offer; he speaks to the entire household of Cornelius, and they believe, receive the gift of the Spirit, and are baptized. As Peter himself says, the Gentiles acceptance of God's Spirit meant baptism could not be denied them (Acts 10:47). These events were reported to the Jerusalem apostles, whose natural prejudices were overcome; they concluded, "God has also given the Gentiles repentance for life" (11:18).

Acts describes Peter as reaching out to Gentiles who acknowledged and respected the Torah of Moses without accepting the covenant of circumcision that was binding on Jews. Cornelius is described as "pious and fearing God with all his house" (Acts 10:2). The term "God-fearer" or "God-worshipper" was used of Gentiles who acknowledged the God of Israel without accepting all the commandments that Moses gave the Israelites. Cornelius' emissaries to Peter underscore this description by saying he is "a just man, both fearing God and attested by all the nation of the Jews" (10:22). His prophetic experience causes Peter to conclude that God does not discriminate, but that "in every nation the one who fears him and does justice is acceptable to him" (10:35).

In the book of Acts, the presentation of God-fearers as models of faith in Christ among Gentiles has its clearest expression in chapter 15, the third time that the prophetic narrative concerning Peter features. Peter declares that, since God gave his Holy Spirit to Gentiles who believed, no attempt should be made to add the requirement of circumcision to them (Acts 15:6–11). He makes this statement during a meeting with the other recognized apostles of his time. This meeting in Jerusalem set Christianity on a new course.

Peter's view supports the position of two other apostles— Barnabas and Paul—who had recently come from Antioch, where many Gentiles had also been baptized. In the opinion of some disciples, described by Acts as "some who believed from the school of the Pharisees" (15:5), the commandment of circumcision had to be kept by those who had been baptized. Their teaching made good sense, because in the written Torah God explicitly gives Abraham circumcision as "the sign of the covenant" for all his posterity (Genesis 17:10–14).

In this case, Jesus' movement confronted the issue of whether to see the Torah as the center of ethics, or Prophecy as the controlling influence in behavior. The tension between those choices had been implicit since the time that Jesus claimed that his preaching of God's Kingdom put love, rather than the Torah, at the center of ethical concern. The resurrection confirmed the sense of the prophetic empowerment of all who received the Spirit, no matter what their background according to the Torah. The choice of whether or not to insist on the covenant of circumcision, required by the Torah and yet suspended by Peter in the house of Cornelius, heightened that tension to the point that a decision had to be made.

The apostles Peter, Paul, and Barnabas are on the side of Prophecy in Acts 15. The move from Torah to Prophecy as the ethical center of the movement had already been made by the end of Jesus' life, and his resurrection opened the view of baptism as a means of access to God's Spirit opened to all flesh.

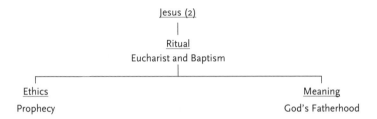

But the followers of Jesus, before and after his death, did not function as scholars of religion, and the difference between what we now call Judaism and what we now call Christianity was not understood as a matter of course. Jesus never rejected the Torah; he famously claimed to fulfill it (Matthew 5:17). But that fulfillment involved extending, adapting, reinterpreting, and applying it in radically new ways, following the prophetic prompting of the love commandment as the fulfillment of God's Kingdom.

Controversy concerning circumcision and the related question of the extent to which the Torah should regulate how Gentile believers should conduct themselves did not really end with one meeting in Jerusalem (as the book of Acts implies). Nor did it result in complete agreement. A group of Christians known as the Ebionites (from the word for "poor" in Hebrew) continued to keep the covenant of circumcision until they were absorbed by Muslim expansion during the seventh century CE.

Yet the outcome of the meeting in Jerusalem in 46 CE, known as the Jerusalem Council, proved determinative in the practice of Christianity as a whole in regard to circumcision. Acts sets out the definitive position, not as Peter's, but by quoting James, the eldest of Jesus' four brothers (see Mark 6:3). James was widely respected for his piety by the population as a whole in Jerusalem and came to be the guide of Jesus' followers there. In the account of Acts James confirms the view of Peter, but he states the position in a new way: "Symeon [he says, using Peter's real name] has related how God first visited the Gentiles, to take a people in his name" (Acts 15:14). James' perspective here is that in addition to Israel God has established a people in his name. How the new people are to be regarded in relation to Israel is a question that underlies the statement, and James goes on to provide an answer.

JAMES, THE BROTHER OF JESUS

James is listed at the head of Jesus' brothers in the Synoptic Gospels, in a statement of a crowd in Nazareth that is skeptical that one whose family they know can be responsible for wonders (Mark 6:1–6; Matthew 13:53–58). In John's Gospel, he is among the brothers who argued with Jesus about his refusal to go to Jerusalem for a feast (John 7:2–10), and James is also referred to anonymously as among the brothers whom, even with his mother, Jesus refused to interrupt his teaching in order to greet (Mark 3:31–35; Matthew 12:46–50; Luke 8:19–21). James and his family are marginalized by such references, so that tension with Jesus is implied.

Despite Jesus' troubles with his family, Acts attributes to James (and to James alone) the power to decide whether non-Jewish male converts to Christianity needed to be circumcised. He determines that they do not, but proceeds to command them to observe certain requirements of purity (so Acts 15:1–35). That explains why emissaries from James make their appearance as villains in Paul's description of a major controversy at Antioch. They insisted on a separate meal-fellowship of Jews and non-Jews, while Paul with equal insistence (but apparently little or no success) argued for the unity of Jewish and non-Jewish fellowship within the Church (Galatians 2:11–12:21). How James came to such a position of prominence is not explained in Acts, although Paul does refer to James as a witness of Jesus' resurrection (1 Corinthians 15:7), and the non-canonical *Gospel according to the Hebrews* (approvingly cited by Jerome, *Liber de Viris Illustribus* 2) presents a full account of his fasting before his vision.

James develops the relationship between those taken from the Gentiles and Israel by the use of Scripture. He claims that "with this [that is, his statement of Peter's position] the words of the prophets agree, just as it is written" (Acts 15:15), and he goes on to cite from the book of Amos. As James has it, there is actual agreement between Symeon and the words of the prophets, as two people might agree: the use of the verb *sumphoneo* underscores this idea. The direct continuity of Christian experience with Scripture is a marked feature of James' view.

The citation from Amos (9:11–12, from the version of the Septuagint which was the Bible of Luke–Acts) comports well with James' concern that the position of the Church agree with the principal vocabulary of the prophets (Acts 15:16–17):

After this I will come back and restore the tent of David that has fallen, and rebuild its ruins and set it up anew, that the rest of men may seek the Lord, and all the Gentiles upon whom my name is called.

In the argument of James as represented here, what the belief of Gentiles achieves is the restoration of the house of David. The argument is possible because a Davidic genealogy of Jesus—and, therefore, of his brother James—is assumed. James contended that Jesus was restoring the house of David because he was the agent of final judgment and was being accepted as such by Gentiles.

James' focus was on Jesus' role as the ultimate arbiter within the Davidic line, and the Temple within this position was the natural place to worship God and acknowledge Jesus. Embracing the Temple as central meant for James, as it meant for the generality of those associated with worship there, maintaining the purity that it was understood that God required in his house. Purity involved excluding Gentiles from the interior courts of the Temple, where Israel was involved in sacrifice. The line of demarcation between Israel and non-Israel was the natural result of seeing Jesus as the triumphant branch of the house of David.

Gentile belief in Jesus was, therefore, in James' understanding a vindication of the house of David as represented by Jesus and by James himself, and it did not involve a fundamental change in the status of Gentiles vis-à-vis Israel. That characterization of the Gentiles, developed by means of the reference to Amos, enabled James to proceed to his requirements of their recognition of purity. (These requirements are set out in Acts 15 as if they were part of the same meeting, but in fact they come from a later council.) He first states that "I determine not to trouble those of the Gentiles who turn to God" (15:19), as if he were simply repeating the policy of Peter in regard to circumcision, although on his own personal authority as representing the house of David. But he then continues that his determination is also "to write to them to abstain from the pollutions of the idols, and from fornication, and from what is strangled, and from blood" (15:20).

THE COUNCIL OF JERUSALEM

In two meetings in Jerusalem that determined Christian ritual policy for years to come (in 46 CE and 52 CE), James, the brother of Jesus, came to two findings. The first was that Gentile believers were not required to keep the covenant of circumcision as part of their baptism. The second was that they nonetheless needed to keep certain requirements of ritual purity that were designed to preserve recognition of the Torah. The rules set out by James in Acts 15:20 tended naturally to separate believing Gentiles from their ambient environment. They are to refrain from feasts in honor of the gods and from foods sacrificed to idols in the course of being butchered and sold. (The notional devotion of animals in the market to one god or another was a common practice in the Hellenistic world.) They are to observe stricter limits than usual on the type of sexual activity they might engage in, and with whom. (Gross promiscuity need not be the only issue here; marriage to relatives is also included within the area of concern. That was fashionable in the Hellenistic world and proscribed in the book of Leviticus (see chapter 18 and 20:17–21)). They are to avoid the flesh of animals that had been strangled instead of bled, and they are not to consume blood itself. The proscription of blood, of course, was basic in Judaism; and strangling an animal (as distinct from cutting its throat) increased the availability of blood in the meat. Such strictures are consistent with James' initial observation that God had taken a people from the Gentiles (15:14); they were to be similar to Israel and supportive of Israel in their distinction from the Hellenistic world at large.

The motive behind the rules is not separation in itself, however. James links them to the fact that the Mosaic legislation regarding purity is well and widely known (15:21):

For Moses from early generations has had those preaching him city by city, being read in the synagogues every Sabbath.

Because the Law is well known, James insists that believers, even Gentile believers, are not to live in flagrant violation of what Moses enjoined. In the words of Amos, they are to behave as "all the Gentiles upon whom my name is called." As a result of James' insistence, the meeting in Jerusalem sends envoys and a letter to Antioch in order to require Gentiles to honor the prohibitions set out by James (Acts 15:22–35).

James' prohibitions as presented in Acts are designed to show that believing Gentiles honor the law which is commonly read, without in any way changing their status as Gentiles. Thereby, the tent of David is erected again, in the midst of Gentiles who show their awareness of the restoration by means of their respect for the Torah. The interpretation attributed to James involves an application of Davidic vocabulary to Jesus, as is consistent with the claim of Jesus' family to Davidic ancestry. The transfer of Davidic promises to Jesus is accomplished within an acceptance of the terms of reference of the Scripture generally: to embrace David is to embrace Moses.

FACING A HOSTILE EMPIRE

For all the careful argument of James and his followers, the inclusion of non-Jews among believers ran the risk that the Romans would see the movement as a new *superstitio* (a "cult", as people today would say), rather than as practitioners of a *religio licita* (that is, legitimate custom). The very name given to Jesus' followers, *khristianoi*, was a sign of this problem, and of coming trouble.

Adherents of the movement came to be known as "Christians" (meaning partisans of Christ) in Antioch by around the year 45 CE, and they embraced that term of intended ridicule. The use of the term by outsiders highlights the marginal status of non-Jews who accepted baptism. Without conversion to Judaism, they were not Jews in the usual understanding; having rejected the gods of Hellenism by being baptized, they were also no longer at home in the Greco-Roman syncretism that was then fashionable. By calling disciples *khristianoi* (Acts 11:26), a term analogous to *Kaisarianoi* (supporters of Caesar), outsiders compared the movement more to a political faction than to a religion.

This perilous situation for Christians could be exploited by their opponents or by those eager to find scapegoats to deflect hostility from themselves. In the year 64 CE, the Emperor Nero used the marginal status of Christians to get out of a difficult political situation of his own. In that year, a huge fire destroyed Rome, and it was rumored that the conflagration had been set at Nero's order. (There is no doubt that he exploited the opportunity to rebuild the city.) Nero attempted to deflect suspicion from himself by fastening blame for the fire on Christians. They were rounded up, interrogated, and slaughtered, often with elaborate means of torture. Nero's excesses in regard to the Christians were obvious even to those who held that their religion was superstitious.

In Jerusalem, meanwhile, trouble of a different kind was brewing for both Judaism and Christianity. A new spirit of nationalism influenced the priestly aristocracy. Josephus, a Jewish historian of the period who himself lived during this time, began his career as a priestly nationalist and ended it as Rome's protégé. He reports that James, the brother of Jesus, was killed in the Temple in 62 CE at the instigation of the high priest during the interregnum of two Roman governors (*Antiquities* 20 § 197–203). His death dealt a blow to Christianity, but this execution was also ominous for the prospects of Judaism within the empire. Josephus' account of the period makes it clear that from this time on Rome contended with a rising tide of nationalism by resorting to military means.

The tide rose fatefully in the year 66 CE, when Eleazar (the *sagan* or manager of the Temple) convinced priests not to accept any offerings from non-Jews (*Jewish War* 2 § 409). That included the sacrifices paid for by Rome, so the authorities of the Temple were breaching the conditions that made possible Rome's recognition of Judaism as a *religio licita*. Jewish insurgents took the Antonia, the fortress adjacent to the Temple, and killed the Roman soldiers within. War had been irrevocably declared, and the victor could only have been Rome. Consequently the Temple itself was destroyed by fire in 70 CE after a protracted siege.

The period after the Jewish War saw much unrest among Jews outside of geographical Israel, especially during the reign of Trajan (98–117 CE). Trajan also had to deal with the question of what to do with Christians. In a letter written in 111 CE to Pliny, governor of Bithynia and Pontus in Asia Minor, Trajan set out his policy. Recognition of the Roman gods (including the emperor as *divi filius,* son of God) is said by Trajan to be all that should be required of those denounced as Christians. The question was not their profession of Christianity or their practice as such, only whether they were loyal to the empire. By this time, there is no question of simply identifying Christianity with Judaism.

Indeed, the empire may be said to have recognized a separation between Judaism and Christianity before Jews and Christians did. Nero never considered extending the rights of a *religio licita* to Christians in 64 CE, although many followers of Jesus still worshiped in the temple in Jerusalem. Not until around 85 CE would the framers of a principal prayer of Judaism, the Eighteen Benedictions, compose a curse to be included against the Nazoraeans, followers of Jesus. On the Christian side, the claim formally to replace Judaism only came near the end of the first century. Trajan simply takes the separation for granted, in effect treating Christianity as a harmless superstition.

During this period, Christians needed to frame a conception of themselves and of their values that transcended what the Roman

Empire, Jewish authorities, and other religious groups had to say about them. A key to their push back against the marginalization of their faith is given in the correspondence between Trajan and Pliny already mentioned. As governor, Pliny reports that when he interrogated those denounced as Christians, they confessed only to meeting before dawn to sing to Christ "as to a god" and to share a meal. Then they dispersed.

Although Pliny's remarks lack detail, they correspond to the basic pattern of ritual we have already uncovered: baptism and worship in meals of Eucharist. During this period, Christians in Pliny's region began to install their own immersion pools. Before there was any distinctive architecture for a church, which had to await the legalization of Christianity, the baptistery signaled how Christians believed that they entered into a new reality when they were immersed in the name of Christ. As in the case of the Jewish immersion pool (the *miqveh*), one set of steps led in and another set led out. But Christians arranged the steps so that they could descend for baptism at the west and exit—immersed in his name—at the east, toward the sun, a symbol of resurrection.

THE BAPTISMAL CREED

Socially ostracized and sometimes persecuted, Christians saw their identity—as sealed in baptism—as a matter of their relationship to God. That relationship trumped any other. In their practice, they developed what is called in Greek a *sumbolon*, from which the English term "symbol" derives. *Sumbolon* etymologically refers to a throwing together and in Greek conveys how a word, phrase, sign, or statement can invoke a larger set of ideas or relations. At the simplest end of the spectrum of usage, a visual cue might tell you where to find a butcher's shop (of which the symbol was a large hook). At the complex end of the spectrum, Christians set out in their *sumbolon* the pattern of relations to God that baptism involved.

Because those baptized assented to this pattern of faith by affirming their belief, the *sumbolon* came to be called a *credo* in Latin, which means, "I believe." The earliest known version of the *sumbolon* is known in English as the Apostles' Creed.

THE APOSTLES' CREED

The form currently used has developed considerably since the second century. As a guide to its ancient formulation, the best source is the *Apostolic Tradition* of Hippolytus, probably written in 217 CE. Hippolytus sets out the three questions which candidates for baptism answered by saying, *credo*: "I believe."

> Do you believe in God the Father Almighty?
> Do you believe in Christ Jesus the Son of God,
> born of the Holy Spirit of the Virgin Mary,
> and was crucified under Pontius Pilate and was dead and buried
> and rose again on the third day, alive from the dead,
> and ascended into heaven
> and sat on the right hand of the Father
> and will come to judge the living and dead?
> Do you believe in the Holy Spirit
> and the holy Church and the resurrection of the flesh?

The division of the creed into three sections, corresponding to Father, Son, and Spirit, gave rise to the teaching of the Trinity. But the *sumbolon* of baptism does not concern philosophical theology first of all. Later, especially from the fourth century, how the one God needed to be understood as Father, Son, and Spirit without betraying monotheism emerged as a principal preoccupation. But at its point of origin the creed provided believers with a résumé of their own identity and the means to maintain that identity in the midst of a sometimes hostile world.

"Take courage," Jesus says in the Gospel according to John, "I have overcome the world" (John 16:33). In the language of the New Testament and of early Christianity, the "world" (*kosmos*, sometimes also called the "age" from the Greek term *aion*) is the realm of false values, idolatry, and selfishness. Baptism was the moment to transcend that world, first of all by accepting God as one's Father, exactly as Jesus taught. Use of the Aramaic term "*abba*" ("father") in baptism survived long after the transition to Greek as the principal language of Christianity. That practice emphasized the connection to Jesus from the outset of the creed and also served as a reminder that the 'abba is the source of all ("almighty," as the creedal texts say), and therefore transcendent as well as personal.

Jesus takes up the majority of attention in the creed. As the believer calls God "Father," so he or she also learns what it is to be God's "son" (or, more inclusively, "child," a term also used in some texts from the second century). Jesus both derives from God ("of the Holy Spirit") and comes from a human mother ("of the Virgin Mary"). At the time the creed was composed, no single teaching of how Jesus came to be born was accepted. Some believers taught that he was conceived without a human father (see Luke 1:34), but others were convinced that Joseph was Jesus' father, and needed to be, for him to be of the house and lineage of David (see John 1:45). The creed does not take sides in that dispute and does not explain why Jesus died under Pontius Pilate or how he was raised from the dead. The *sumbolon* was designed to bring believers together in a common recognition of Christ, not to settle disputes in regard to differing teachings about him.

For that reason, the closing portion of the statement about Jesus, his ascension, his association with the Father ("on the right hand"), and his role as final judge, appears all the more striking. Taken together with the resurrection, these elements—which deal with Jesus' identity as known after the crucifixion—greatly outweigh the historical assertion that he was born and died. The crucial importance of Christ in the creed turns on who he is, as a heavenly figure, not who he was as an historical figure.

Although believers are to relate to God as their 'abba in the way that Jesus did, they know they are to do that because he is God's Son as the initiator of the whole possibility of this relationship. For that reason, he shares the eternity of the Father, transcending death, inhabiting heaven, sharing the Father's power, and giving divine judgment a human face. A believer who saw the reality of this relationship to God through Christ was equipped to confront the "world" of an unsympathetic Roman Empire.

The last paragraph of the creed, devoted to the Holy Spirit, completes its baptismal association. As in the case of Peter's preaching in the house of Cornelius (see Acts 10:34–48), the coming of the Spirit gives baptism its underlying sense. But in the *sumbolon* the common reception of the Spirit is used to assert the communal nature of life in the Spirit. To be baptized is to share the Spirit with the "Church," a term which originated in Greek to refer to a meeting of people who had been "called out" (*ekklesia*). In this case, the calling out is to the life of the Spirit, with its promise of resurrection for believers. "The resurrection" refers, not to Jesus' resurrection (which has already been mentioned), but to the ultimate destiny of all who believe in him with their full identity (their "flesh").

Paul articulated the teaching on the Spirit of God that the Creed represents. He understands that the Spirit of sonship that raised Jesus from the dead is also available to Jesus' followers in baptism (Romans 8:14–16):

> For as many as are led by God's Spirit, they are God's sons. Because you did not receive a spirit of slavery again, for fear, but you received a spirit of sonship, by which we cried out, *Abba*, Father! The Spirit itself testified with our spirit that we are God's children.

What had begun with the immersion of John and his disciple Jesus, practiced for the purpose of purification, had become something new and distinctive and—in the practice of Christian faith—absolutely fundamental. Baptism now was into Jesus' name for the reception of the Holy Spirit. God's presence was so intimate and commanding that what happened amounted to a "new creation" (so Paul in Galatians 6:15–16). To be immersed into Jesus' name was also to be drenched with the outpouring of God's Spirit, and the social and natural and supernatural changes in the understanding of purity that that involved.

INTERPRETING THE SCRIPTURES

Belief that baptism brought the Spirit of God directly into the hearts of the faithful produced a profound challenge to a conventional reading of the Scripture. We have already seen that James and his circle, speaking authoritatively, found through its interpretation of the prophet Amos that non-Jews who wished to receive baptism might do so, without the additional requirement that they keep the practice of male circumcision. The guiding principle that James in Acts 15 derived from Amos 9:11–12 was that Gentiles were an additional people, added to Israel, so that they should not be required to keep the entire Torah. This meant that Jewish followers of Jesus enjoyed a fundamental privilege.

THE EUCHARIST IN THE CIRCLE OF JAMES

James, the brother of Jesus, saw the Eucharist as a Seder, the meal of the Passover, in terms of both its meaning and its chronology. It being so understood, only Jews in a state of purity could fully participate in the Eucharist, which could be truly recollected only once a year, at Passover in Jerusalem (so Exodus 12:48). During the second century, some disciples insisted that the commemoration of the Last Supper and Easter had to be precisely on the fourteenth day of the Jewish month of Nisan, that is, on Passover. They were called Quartodecimans, and their stance involved decades of controversy. The debate became fierce because it was grounded in contention concerning the nature of Christianity. James' program was to integrate Jesus' movement fully within the liturgical institutions of Judaism and to insist upon the Judaic identity of the movement and upon Jerusalem as its governing center.

Yet James also required that baptized Gentiles should keep certain requirements of the Law in order to honor it as God's revelation to Israel. In this regard, the policy of James ran into direct opposition from the policy of Paul. Their opposition was spelled out over issues of interpretation and in other ways. Unlike James, Paul believed that whenever a person believed in Christ and received the Holy Spirit, that person actually became an Israelite, a son or child of Abraham (Galatians 3:6–9; 6:15–16). People might be Jews or Gentiles by the way they came to the faith, but they came to one faith. His signal prophetic statement sums up his whole position: "There is not any Jew or Greek, not any slave or free, not any male or female, because you are all one in Jesus Christ, and if you are Christ's, then you are Abraham's seed" (Galatians 3:28–29).

PAUL'S EUCHARIST

Paul resisted James' view by insisting Jesus' last meal occurred on the night in which he was betrayed (1 Corinthians 11:23), not on Passover. He emphasizes the link between Jesus' death and the Eucharist, and he agreed with the presentation of the Synoptic Gospels (Mark, Matthew, and Luke) that the heroism of Jesus made the meal into an occasion to join in the solidarity of martyrdom by being willing to suffer for one's faith.

This radical definition of what it meant to be Abraham's progeny and Israel did not represent a consensus in Paul's own time. Far from it. In the same letter to the Galatians in which he spells out his distinctive position for the first time (in the year 53 CE), Paul also admits that his view ran into the vehement disagreement of great apostles before him: James, Peter, and Barnabas. They continued to see Jews and Gentiles as separate, even after baptism, and so they assumed that Jewish dietary laws would mark a line of demarcation between them and that their meals—including Eucharist—would be enjoyed separately. But Paul assumed that children of Abraham and of God's Spirit should eat commonly (especially during Eucharist) and he entered into a face-to-face confrontation with Peter at Antioch over this issue (Galatians 2:11–21). He lost the argument and left Antioch to work in more predominantly Gentile areas.

Even after that confrontation, Paul pursued his disagreement with policies of James as a matter of principle. At an apostolic meeting in Jerusalem in 52 CE, prohibition of food sacrificed to idols for all believers, whether Jews or Gentiles, had been made a requirement. That requirement was kept well into the second century, but Paul resisted it. He insisted that, as he said, "We know that an idol is nothing in the world and that there is no God but one" (I Corinthians 8:4). Consequently, for anyone who has thought through the issue, eating food sacrificed to an idol is a matter of indifference. Paul is careful to specify that believers should avoid any impression of accepting the reality of idols so as not to lead less critical people astray.

While he opposes idolatry in any form, Paul makes the distinction between the object, in itself a harmless statue, and the worship of a spurious divinity. He thinks of reality consistently, along the lines of the physical and the spiritual. His concern is to bring believers to focus on the spiritual. Just as the idol is a physical fact with no purchase on spiritual reality, so Israel is a spiritual fact that cannot be limited to concerns of physical descent.

In regard to these and related issues, Paul argued a minority position in his own time, but as non-Jews came to predominate among believers, his arguments were embraced as the consensus within the Church. He even came to be called "the Apostle" during the second century—as if he had always spoken for the majority. Although James' prohibition against food sacrificed to idols was maintained, Paul's distinction between the objects themselves and the intention of idolatry became received wisdom. And his view that the election of a people went beyond historic Israel became conventional among Christians.

But Paul's massive influence was not merely a matter of the demographic shift that saw Gentile leadership eclipse Jewish leadership in the second century. More importantly, he pioneered an approach to interpreting the Scriptures that became normative. Just as he saw the definition of idols and of Israel in terms of two levels of reality, he believed that the Scriptures of Israel had to be approached with two levels in mind. In his interpretation, Scripture provided the answer to the question of who the true people of God were and what was required of them.

Paul in his letter to the Galatians refers to Ishmael and Isaac in the book of Genesis (chapters 16 and 21), the one born to a slave (Hagar) and the other to a free woman (Sarah). Paul asserts that these two sons of Abraham are not only figures from the past but also allegories, referring to those born of slavery as contrasted with those born for promise (Galatians 4:21–31). The Spirit comes to those who understand that Scripture promises to transcend all forms of servitude, because those who accept baptism are like Isaac, born of a free woman.

In making this comparison, Paul insists that the Torah exists principally in order to prophesy the coming of the Spirit. When it refers to rules about ordinary living (which Paul calls "the flesh"), that is to point forward to spiritual realities. For him, the fundamental purpose of the Torah is to serve as a form of prophecy. He assumes that it will continue as binding on the practice of Judaism, but he does not believe that an acceptance of Judaism, even in a reduced form, is necessary for baptism. The people of God are Isaac, not Ishmael, and the essential function of the Torah is to prophesy, not to regulate behavior.

For this reason, when Paul looks back to the exodus from Egypt and the founding events of Israel, in his mind they refer to present, spiritual realities. Passing through the Red Sea was a baptism, and discovering food and water in the wilderness was spiritual food such as believers share in the Eucharist. These providential events of the past are, in Paul's language, "types" (1 Corinthians 10:1–6). By using this term, he expressed his understanding of the prophetic meaning of the Torah and of all Scripture with a concept familiar in the popular Greek philosophy of his time.

The word "type" (*tupos*) itself refers to a mold that one might make to cast a statue. (In later technology, this provided us with the language of typefaces and typewriters.) In the philosophy of Plato that deeply influenced the Greek-speaking world of Paul's time, the world around us is made up of types. What we perceive is not reality itself, but the physical molds of ideal or spiritual forms. When Paul says the events of the exodus of Israel out of Egypt are "types," he means that what happened in the past realizes its full meaning only in the present, with the coming of the Spirit to believers in order to make them the children of God. Although Paul's language was recognizable as Platonic, his usage was also prophetic.

Prophetic typology became characteristic of Christian interpretation of Scripture from the second century on and remains one of Paul's distinctive contributions to the Church. But once made, his contribution acquired a life all its own.

A theologian of the second century, Justin Martyr, turned Paul's prophetic typology into a comprehensive philosophy of how human beings can know God. The added dimension of Justin's approach came from his use of the motif of Jesus as the *logos* or "word" of God in the Gospel according to John (John 1:1–18). Here Jesus is much more than a historical figure. Rather, he embodies the plan of God at the creation: "In the beginning was the word and the word was with God and the word was God" (John 1:1). The thought behind this idea is that God needed to have a design or logic in mind in order to frame the world, and because human beings are in the image and likeness of God

(Genesis 1:26–27), the original archetype from which the world derives as its type must be human. As John puts it, "the *logos* became flesh and dwelt among us" (1:14), known as Jesus Christ. He embodies a primordial and eternal reality.

Justin Martyr thought that this conception of the *logos*, although applicable to Scripture, included all human understanding that truly knows God. To Justin's way of thinking, all authentic insight into the divine derives from the *logos*, so that even Socrates is a prophet of the *logos* "in which the whole human race partakes" (*Apology* 46.2). Universal though this conception is in its scope, Justin is also very clear that Christians enjoy its focused reality. Speaking of the Eucharist, he says (*Apology* 66.2):

> Because we do not take as ordinary bread or ordinary drink, but in the same way as through God's *Logos* Jesus Christ our incarnate savior had flesh and blood for our salvation, so also the food given thanks for through an oath of a *logos* from him, from which our blood and flesh are nourished by assimilation, is—we have learned—the flesh and blood of that incarnate Jesus.

THE EUCHARIST IN EARLY CHRISTIANITY

Justin Martyr was inspired not only by the Johannine *logos*, but also by John's understanding of the Eucharist. In John's presentation Jesus identified himself as the *manna*, miraculous food bestowed by God upon his people (Exodus 16). John understands the Eucharist as a Mystery, in which Jesus offers his own flesh and blood (John 6:30–35, 41–58). That autobiographical reading of Jesus' words—as giving his personal body and blood in Eucharist—represents a consciously non-Judaic and Hellenistic development. It involves participants in joining by oath (*sacramentum* in Latin, corresponding to *musterion* in the Greek vocabulary of primitive Christianity) in the sacrifice of the mysterious hero, separating themselves from others. Eucharist has become sacrament and involves a knowing conflict with the ordinary understanding of what Judaism might and might not include.

Justin argued against any other understanding of the Scriptures, and specifically a Jewish understanding, as being literal. How aware Justin was of Jewish teaching, in particular in its Rabbinic form, remains unclear. Yet anyone who is familiar with the development of Judaism from the second century onward will appreciate the irony of his understanding of Judaic interpretation. The second century was just the period when Scripture was being interpreted within Judaism in terms of its eternal meaning, when any limitation on its immediate reference came to be overridden by an appeal to the significance of the eternal Torah. Both Judaism and Christianity made the immediate reference of Scripture ancillary to its systemic significance. But because Christianity was committed to the *Logos* as its systemic center, and Judaism to the Torah as its systemic center, the two could not understand one another.

Justin is committed to a typological reading of Scripture, the Christian norm during the second century. The prophets were understood to represent "types" of Christ, impressions on their minds of the heavenly reality, God's own son. By the end of the century, Christians such as Clement of Alexandria and Tertullian called any limitation on the immediate reference of Scripture (its "literal meaning") the "Jewish sense."

While Paul famously still hoped that "all Israel will be saved" (Romans 11:26), Justin is categorical that "there is to be an ultimate Law and Covenant superior to all, which now must be kept by all people who claim God's inheritance" (*Dialogue with Trypho* 11.2–3). This eternal covenant (Isaiah 55:3–4) establishes who is a true, spiritual Israelite and who is not (*Dialogue with Trypho* 11.5), taking the place of all other aspirants to that identity.

A key reason for Christianity's claim to supersede Judaism was the conviction that the typological reading of Israel's Scriptures, and *only* that reading, uncovered their true meaning. God's Spirit stood behind the utterances of the prophets, but they looked ahead to a fulfillment beyond their own times and conditions. Those who saw this fulfillment in Christ naturally tended to see the Scriptures of Israel as the Old Covenant or Old Testament: a book of types. The reality from which those types derived was Christ, and the books that attested Christ directly took the name of the New Testament.

Some Christians during the second, third, and fourth centuries believed that the reality of Christ so thoroughly transcended the

Scriptures of Israel that the Old Testament could be dispensed with. After all, if circumcision and many laws of purity could be ignored, why not the Torah generally? Indeed, a few groups believed that the Old Testament spoke of a false god who was jealous of the true Father of all. Today these groups are called "Gnostic," from the Greek term for "knowledge" (*gnosis*). Although it is true that those who wanted to dispense with the Scriptures and even the God of Israel styled themselves as "Gnostic," many believers of all kinds did so as well. The creed that one embraced at baptism, after all, conveyed insights about God, and every believer laid claim to the illuminating Spirit of God in Christ.

Yet it is true that those who wished to dispense with the revelation to Israel, seeing it replaced by the revelation through Christ, did set their knowledge (*gnosis*) above the inherited chain of tradition that had brought Christ to them. Their views were disputed by groups known as "catholic," a term also derived from Greek (*katholikos*) that means "universal" (literally, "through the whole" or "for the whole"). Catholics defined the emerging faith in terms of belief and practice throughout the Church in the world as they knew it. To them, the Old Testament provided the indispensable language of types that made understanding Christ possible.

The Old Testament as embraced by Catholics was essentially the Greek Bible used in Judaism, rendered from Aramaic and Hebrew originals from the third century BCE. It was known as the Septuagint, because seventy translators allegedly produced the rendering. This Jewish Bible was accepted as authoritative by major teachers in Judaism, although it included works in Greek that had no counterpart in the Hebrew Bible that the Rabbis canonized. Additional works of this kind, known as apocryphal, include the Wisdom of Solomon and the books of the Maccabees. This version of the Old Testament was so influential that it is the text usually cited, rather than the Hebrew, in the New Testament and early Christian theology and is the basis of versions of the Old Testament in many other languages in the ancient world.

Together with readings of the Old Testament, Christians in their worship also read what Justin called the "memoirs of the apostles" (*Apology* 67.3). By the second century, this amounted to a collection almost identical to what we know of as the New Testament. Although oral tradition was the almost exclusive medium of instruction in Jesus' movement during his lifetime, Paul wrote letters to congregations he had founded or contacted. Paul was able to call upon the work of secretaries, and a network developed during his career for the circulation and preservation of what he wrote. Those letters became the basis of a collection of writings which were supplemented by his followers after his death.

The existence of Paul's letters provided an incentive for the emergence of the Gospels. Their sources go back to apostolic teachers such as Peter, Barnabas, James, and the group of disciples in Jerusalem who looked to James for leadership. Their teachings about Jesus were brought together in order to instruct converts to Christianity before baptism. When these oral materials were put into Greek and used in centers of the new faith such as Damascus, Rome, and Antioch, and then emerged as written documents, they looked very similar to one another, and yet each—Matthew, Mark, and Luke—is distinctive. These three Gospels can be "seen together" (and so are called the Synoptic Gospels) in the sense that they can be compared page by page, and form a unique genre of writing. They are called "Gospels" from the terms in Greek (*euanggelion*) and Aramaic (*besorta'*) that refer to an announcement of victory. Jesus had used this term of his heralding of God's Kingdom (see Mark 1:15), and to this day "gospel" refers to his message, and "Gospel" is used to speak of the books concerning him.

The precedent of Paul's letters provoked the composition of letters named after different teachers, and the Synoptic Gospels encouraged the production of other Gospels. Of the dozens of additional Gospels available in antiquity, only the Gospel according to John came to stand with the others in what is called the canon of the New Testament. The term canon means "measure" or "standard," and came to refer among Catholic believers to those works that both derived from apostolic teaching and were used throughout the Church. Those parameters excluded works that were known to be the purely personal teaching of recent local teachers.

As early as the second century, thinkers such as Irenaeus saw a providential significance in the shape of the canon (*Refutation of False Knowledge* 3.11.8):

> Since there are four zones of the world in which we live, and four principal winds, while the Church is spread over all the earth, and the pillar

and foundation of the Church are the gospel, and the Spirit of life, it fittingly has four pillars, everywhere breathing out incorruption and revivifying men. From this it is clear that the Word, the artificer of all things, being manifested to men gave us the gospel, fourfold in form but held together by one Spirit.

In a single, elegant statement, Irenaeus expressed the relationship between the Gospels as documents and the gospel message of Jesus, who emerges as the divine principle behind the universe as a whole.

CHURCH

Although the contents of the canon were largely agreed during the second century, several works remained controversial for two centuries after. Only then did the definitive canon of twenty-seven books of the New Testament emerge. The two works that produced the most controversy, because they stretched the usual standard of what makes a book canonical, reflect the deepest concerns of the Church during the period.

The Epistle to the Hebrews was written after Paul's death, and although Paul is the alleged author, it was obvious to most critical observers that its entire approach and style belonged to someone else. The third-century theologian Origen once rhetorically remarked, "Who wrote this epistle? God knows who wrote this epistle!" Despite that doubt, by 367 CE, the influential bishop Athanasius of Alexandria fully accepted the book as canonical, just as he embraced the last book in the New Testament, the Revelation to John, although scholars in Alexandria had long known that it was not written by the same person who wrote the Gospel according to John.

It was vitally important for Athanasius that, in the Revelation, Jesus is portrayed as the Lamb of God who is worshipped in heaven along with the Father (Revelation 5:13). Athanasius championed the emerging doctrine of the Trinity, according to which Jesus as God's Son needed to be seen as of the same essence (*ousia*) as the Father. To him, the Revelation demonstrated that truth. In addition, at the time of Athanasius the Revelation was not seen, as it is today, as being an apocalyptic calendar of disaster and warfare. Instead, educated Christians at that time believed that they were living during the millennium referred to in Revelation 20:3. With Jesus' resurrection, Satan was already bound, the saints ruled, and their influence was as dramatic as a resurrection of its own (Revelation 20:1–5).

Together with this view of the triumphant power of the Church, Athanasius found in the Epistle to the Hebrews a view of Christology that suited the Trinity. Scripture is held to show that the Son and the Son's announcement of salvation are superior to the angels and their message (1:1–2:18; see especially 2:1–4). Jesus is also portrayed as superior to Moses and Joshua, who did not truly bring those who left Egypt into the rest promised by God (3:1–4:13). Having set up a general assertion of the Son's superiority on the basis of Scripture, the author proceeds to his main theme (4:14): "Having, then, a great high priest who has passed into the heavens, Jesus the son of God, let us hold the confession fast." That statement is the key to the central argument of Hebrews.

The key term in the statement is used freshly and—on first acquaintance with the Epistle—somewhat unexpectedly. Jesus, whom we have known as Son, is now "great high priest." The term "high priest" is in fact used earlier, to speak of his having removed sin (2:17), and in that role Jesus is also called the "apostle and high priest of our confession" (3:1). But now, in 4:14, Jesus is the "great high priest," whose position is heavenly. Faith in his heavenly location is the only means to obtain divine mercy: "Let us then draw near with assurance to the throne of grace, so that we might receive mercy and find grace in time of need" (4:16). Hebrews presents Jesus as the unique means of access to God in the only sanctuary that matters, the divine throne in heaven.

The portrayal of Jesus as the great high priest, exalted in heaven, provides the central theme of the Epistle (Hebrews, chapters 4–7). The argument may seem abstruse, turning as it does on Melchizedek, a relatively obscure figure in Genesis 14. In Genesis, Abram is met by Melchizedek after his defeat of the king of Elam. Melchizedek is identified as king of Salem, and as priest of God Most High (Genesis 14:18). He brings bread and wine, and blesses Abram; in return, Abram gives Melchizedek one tenth of what he has in hand after the victory (Genesis 14:18–20).

The author of Hebrews hammers out a principle and a corollary from this narrative. First, "It is beyond all dispute that the lesser is blessed by the greater" (Hebrews 7:7). From that straightforward assertion, the superiority of Melchizedek to Levitical priests is deduced. Levi, the founding father of the priesthood, was still in Abram's loins at the time Abram paid his tithe (a proportion of one tenth) to Melchizedek. In that sense, the Levitical priests who were to receive tithes were themselves tithed by the greater priest (Hebrews 7:8–10).

The importance of Melchizedek to the author of Hebrews, of course, is that he resembles Jesus, the Son of God. His very name means "king of righteousness," and he is also "king of peace," Salem. He does not bear a genealogy, and his birth and death are not recorded (Hebrews 7:2b–4). In all these details, he anticipates Jesus, the true king of righteousness and peace, from a descent that is not priestly in a Levitical sense, but of whom David prophesied in the Psalms, "You are a priest for ever, after the order of Melchizedek" (Hebrews 7:11–25, citing Psalm 110:4 on several occasions; cf. 7:11, 15, 17, 21). Jesus is the guarantor by God's own promise of a better, everlasting covenant (7:22). His surety is linked to Melchizedek's as clearly as the bread and wine which both of them use as the seal of God's promise and blessing.

The superiority of the better covenant is spelled out in what follows in Hebrews through chapter 9, again relying on the attachment to Jesus of God's promise in Psalm 110 (Hebrews 7:28): "For the law appoints men having weakness as high priests, but the word of the oath which is after the law appoints a son for ever perfected." Perfection implies that daily offerings are beside the point. The Son's sacrifice was perfect "once for all, when he offered himself up" (7:26–27). The author leaves nothing to implication: Moses' prescriptions for the sanctuary were a pale imitation of the heavenly sanctuary that Jesus has actually entered (8:1–6). Accordingly, the covenant mediated by Jesus is "better," the "second" replacing the "first," the "new" replacing what is now "obsolete" (8:6–13). As God's Son, Jesus is superior to any other mediator (Hebrews 1:1–4).

With this emphasis on Jesus' status as God's Son, pioneered in Hebrews and elevated to a philosophical doctrine by Athanasius, it is plain that by the fourth century, Christianity had passed through another systemic shift. Seeing Jesus as the Son of God and Logos, Athanasius embraced the teaching of the Council of bishops at

Nicea in Asia Minor and of subsequent councils, which declared that Jesus was "the only-begotten Son of God, begotten of the Father before all worlds, Light of Light, very God of very God, begotten, not made, being of one substance with the Father, by whom all things were made."

THE NICENE CREED

The Emperor Constantine convened a council of leaders of the Church that met at Nicea in Asia Minor in 325 CE. In the midst of a war for the imperial throne Constantine had decided not to persecute Christianity, reversing the policy of Diocletian. The contemporary Christian historian Eusebius celebrated the Edict of Milan, which Constantine issued with Licinius, his ally in the east of the empire, in 313 CE. The Edict signaled the victory of both apology and martyrdom, but the story that Eusebius attached to Constantine's decision heralded events to come.

According to Eusebius, Constantine had a vision before his decisive battle against Maxentius at the Milvian Bridge. He saw a cross in heaven and heard a voice that said, "By this sign, conquer." As a result, he permitted his soldiers to attach Christian signs, presumably crosses, to their shields.

Politically, Constantine's move was astute, in that it enabled him to claim the allegiance of growing numbers of Christians in the Roman Empire, perhaps amounting to some ten percent of the population by his time. Psychologically, his vision and his decision are also explicable, since his mother Helena, the concubine of his father Constantius, was a Christian.

The council addressed the most controversial issue of Christian theology at that time: the relationship between Jesus and God. The depth of the controversy may be measured by the fact that the wording of this Creed, which became standard within the Eucharistic worship of the Catholic, Orthodox Church, was not canonized until the Council of Ephesus in 431 after revision at the council of Constantinople in 381 CE (where the paragraph on the Holy Spirit was added).

Should Jesus be regarded as fully equal in divinity to his Father, the creator of the universe, or should he be seen as subordinate to the Father? This dispute was fierce, because it combined in one argument two difficult areas of contention. First, it obviously raises doubts about the belief in one God to think of Jesus being equal to the Father. But secondly, unless God has in some way actually taken on human flesh, humanity would have little hope of ever attaining eternal life with God.

The Council adopted the principle that Father and Son are equal in their divinity. This new orthodoxy paved the way for the doctrine of the Trinity to emerge, according to which Father, Son, and Spirit are all united in their commonly divine being, although each has a distinctive character. The Council of Chalcedon in 451 CE applied the Creed to the Christological controversies of its time by saying:

> We all with one voice teach the confession of one and the same Son, our Lord Jesus Christ: the same perfect in divinity and perfect in humanity, the same truly God and truly man, of a rational soul and a body; consubstantial with the Father as regards his divinity, and the same consubstantial with us as regards his humanity; like us in all respects except for sin; begotten before the ages from the Father as regards his divinity, and in the last days the same for us and for our salvation from Mary, the virgin God-bearer as regards his humanity; one and the same Christ, Son, Lord, only-begotten, acknowledged in two natures which undergo no confusion, no change, no division, no separation; at no point was the difference between the natures taken away through the union, but rather the property of both natures is preserved and comes together into a single person and a single subsistent being; he is not parted or divided into two persons, but is one and the same only-begotten Son, God, Word, Lord Jesus Christ, just as the prophets taught from the beginning about him, and as the Lord Jesus Christ himself instructed us, and as the creed of the fathers handed it down to us.

Jesus, as before all things, was the principle behind the world, and before the Torah. When the Old Testament spoke, its fulfillment was to be found in the New Testament, and its true meaning could only be understood through Christ, who gave all prophecy from the outset. To Catholic theologians throughout this period, the second-century Epistle of Barnabas, non-canonical but widely respected, was right when it insisted about the commandments of the Torah that "Moses received them being a servant, but the Lord himself gave them to us to be the people of his inheritance, having endured patiently for our sakes" (*Epistle of Barnabas* 14:4)

THE TRINITY

During the fourth century, Gregory of Nyssa in Asia Minor (modern Turkey) developed an influential articulation of the Trinity. Gregory explains that the definition of Father, Son, and Spirit is not established from the point of view of the relation between God and humanity, but on the basis of the relations among the three within Godhead, in the interior of their unique nature: "The character of the superintending and beholding power is one, in Father, Son, and Holy Spirit," such that divine action can be conceived of as "issuing from the Father as from a spring, brought into operation by the Son, and perfecting its grace by the power of the Spirit." Understood in this way, "no operation is separated in respect of the Persons, being fulfilled by each individually apart from that which is joined with him in our contemplation, but all providence, care, and superintendence of all, alike of things in the sensible creation and of those of supramundane nature, and that power which preserves the things which are, and corrects those which are amiss, and instructs those which are ordered aright, is one, and not three, being, indeed, directed by the Holy Trinity." With this formulation, Gregory of Nyssa in his treatise *That there are not three Gods* developed a conception of the Trinity that was metaphysically consistent, coordinated with a teaching of providential care, and suitable for contemplation.

Because Jesus was the true source of all law, law itself could be elevated to a new importance, provided it was interpreted in a

Christological manner. The Ten Commandments, given on tablets of the law before the children of Israel had rebelled against God in the wilderness, were understood to guide believers, but their meaning could only be known in Christ. The day of the Sabbath, for example, no longer could be literally counted as the seventh day that finished the material creation (as in Genesis 2:2–3), but needed to be kept as the day of resurrection, a new spiritual creation.

The principles of ethics, therefore, were no longer to be found directly in prophecy, as at the earliest stage of Christianity, but in the permanent revelation of Jesus as God's Son, the same yesterday, today, forever (Hebrews 13:8), and sanctioned by the Holy Spirit. Once Jesus' Sonship became the fulcrum of ethics, his reality in heaven, at the right hand of God, was taken to provide a template for behavior within the Church. One theologian and famous martyr, Ignatius of Antioch, took the role of priests in the Church to compare with that of Christ. They were owed obedience by their people, and at the same time the priest owed his loyalty to his bishop, as to God.

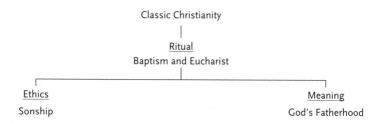

The relationship among the leaders of the Church is an example of how typology became a principle of authority. At its origin, the English term "priest" reflects the Greek *presbuteros*, which means "elder." (In both Hebrew and in Greek, a different term, *kohen* and *hiereus* respectively, referred to the agent of literal sacrifice.) In the first churches, as in synagogues, the elder was expected to give order to the local congregation according to the traditions known to him. Typology, however, turned this role into a reflection of the Son's authority as well as of his obedience.

Similarly, the term "bishop" (Greek *episkopos*) initially referred to the secular role of a manager or overseer in any community and was applied to those in congregations who had charge of communal resources. Once those resources grew with Rome's recognition of Christianity as a legitimate religion, the role of bishop naturally became preeminent. As a result, another name of a Christian leader, "deacon" (from the ordinary Greek word for a servant, *diakonos*) came to signify an ancillary role in relation to the newly managerial bishop. Typology and a changed political climate produced the distinctive threefold ministry of bishop, priest, and deacon that characterized classic Christianity.

The crucial role of Constantine in fomenting the power of Christian clergy was endorsed by Christian theologians, and they sanctified him with typology. Eusebius, a bishop at Nicea and the first extant historian of the early Church, compared the emperor to Christ himself: "Our Emperor, beloved of God, bearing a kind of image of the supreme rule as it were in imitation of the greater, directs the course of all things upon earth" (Eusebius, *Praise of Constantine* 1.6). In this theology, the Roman Empire, an extension of the rule of the saints, joins the Church, as the millennial breakthrough of God's Spirit against Satan, in order to bring the truth and the authority of God to the earth.

The combined imperial and religious power quickly became the preserve of the Roman emperor, acting in accordance with the teaching of the Church. It was entirely natural by the end of the fourth century for the Emperor Theodosius to issue an edict that directed policy toward religious groups on theological grounds:

> According to the apostolic teaching and the doctrine of the Gospel, let us believe the one deity of the Father, the Son, and the Holy Spirit, in equal majesty and in a holy Trinity. We authorize the followers of this law to assume the title of Catholic Christians; but as for the others, since, in our judgment, they are foolish madmen, we decree that they shall be branded with the ignominious name of heretics and shall not presume to give to their conventicles the name of churches.

A single, typologically grounded authority seemed to direct all affairs on earth according to the wisdom vouchsafed from heaven. The continuing rule of the saints seemed in theory to be secure. But less than two decades after Theodosius' edict, one of those heretics—Alaric the Goth, who, although a Christian, did not accept that Jesus as God's Son was equal to God—sacked the city of Rome. The Church believed faith was eternal, but its fate seemed tied up with material challenges, and the situation required an answer. Medieval Christianity developed a response.

SUMMARY

In this chapter we have seen how Classic Christianity emerged:

- By focusing on baptism as the means by which all persons, not merely Israelites, might be integrated in Christ as the Son of God, early Christians presented Judaism as a preparation for the access of all humanity to God's Spirit.
- The first creed of Christianity defined the experience of God in terms of Father, Son, and Spirit.
- The Eucharist came to be seen as putting believers in the presence of Christ, who was also revealed typologically in the Old Testament.
- Christ, indeed, was the *Logos*, the agent and design of all creation, such that people throughout the ages could know him.
- Only the Church, however, enjoyed full knowledge of him in his relation to God as Father and Spirit, with whom the Son formed the eternal Trinity.

FURTHER READING

Brown, Peter (2008) *The Body and Society. Men, Women, and Sexual Renunciation in Early Christianity* (New York: Columbia University Press).

Chadwick, Henry (2001) *The Church in Ancient Society. From Galilee to Gregory the Great* (Oxford: Oxford University Press).

Chilton, Bruce (2004) *Rabbi Paul. An Intellectual Biography* (New York: Doubleday).

Freeman, Charles (2009) *A New History of Early Christianity* (New Haven, CT: Yale University Press).

Kelly, J. N. D. (2006) *Early Christian Creeds* (London: Continuum).

Lang, Bernhard (1997) *Sacred Games. A History of Christian Worship* (New Haven, CT: Yale University Press).

Pelikan, Jaroslav (2003) *Credo. Historical and Theological Guide to Creeds and Confessions of Faith in the Christian Tradition* (New Haven, CT: Yale University Press).

BASICS IN THE MIDDLE AGES
ECONOMIES OF SALVATION

The loss of Rome to Alaric in 410 CE did not by any means spell the end of the Roman Empire. Augustine, Catholic bishop of Hippo in North Africa, even taught—as he lay dying in 430 and his city was besieged by the Vandals—that humanity currently lived in the thousand-year rule of the saints, the millennium predicted in the Revelation of John (20:4; see Augustine, *City of God* 20.9).

In his millennial expectation, as well as in his commitment to sacred violence and its use against "heretics, Jews, and pagans" (Sermon 62.18), Augustine represents a crucial transition to medieval thought in the West. He articulated a rationalization for violence, on the grounds that it was improving for its victims, encouraging the anti-Semitic polemics of his age and providing a moral opportunity to inject zeal into persecution.

Even as this world was made into a field where God's righteousness might be realized, the power of sin—evident in the victory of Alaric—also impressed itself on thinkers such as Augustine. His formulation in *The City of God* became classic. From the outset, he sounds his theme, that the City of God is an eternal city that exists in the midst of the cities of men; those two cities are both mixed and at odds in this world, but they are to be separated by the final judgment (*City of God* 1.1). That thesis is sustained through an account of Roman religion and Hellenistic philosophy, including Augustine's critical appreciation of Plato (books 1–10).

In the central section of his work, Augustine sets out his case within a discussion of truly global history, from the story of the creation in Genesis. From the fall of the angels, which Augustine associates with the separation of light and darkness in Genesis 1:4, he speaks of the striving between good and evil. But the distinction between those two is involved with the will of certain angels, not with any intrinsic wickedness (*City of God* 11.33). People, too, are disordered in their desire, rather than in their creation by God (*City of God* 12.8).

The difference between the will God intends for his creatures and the will they actually evince attests the freedom involved in divine creation. But the effect of perverted will, whether angelic or human, is to establish two antithetical regimes (*City of God* 14.28):

> So two loves have constituted two cities—the earthly is formed by love of self even to contempt of God, the heavenly by love of God even to contempt of self. For the one glories in herself, the other in the Lord. The one seeks glory from man; for the other God, the witness of the conscience, is the greatest glory. ... In the one the lust for power prevails, both in her own rulers and in the nations she subdues; in the other all serve each other in charity, governors by taking thought for all and subjects by obeying.

By book 18, Augustine arrives at his own time and repeats that the two cities "alike enjoy temporal goods or suffer temporal ills, but differ in faith, in hope, in love, until they be separated by the final judgment and each receive its end, of which there is no end" (*City of God* 18.54).

Even now, in the power of the Catholic Church, God is represented on earth, and the present Christian epoch *(Christiana tempora)* corresponds to the millennium promised in Revelation 20 (*City of God* 20.9). This age of dawning power, released in flesh by Jesus and conveyed by the Church, simply awaits the full transition into the city of God, complete with flesh itself.

The sense of Christ's hegemony in the present was celebrated even more confidently in the East, where the depiction of Christ as the conquering *pantokrator* ("all-ruling"), a title applied in the Revelation of John, became a focal icon and theological concept.

Constantine had already moved his capital from Rome to Byzantium in 330 CE, vastly enlarging the city and renaming it Constantinople. This was the new Rome, and its location was better than the old Rome's from the point of view of trade and commerce. Moreover, Constantine and his successors were better able to confront the greatest alternative power of their time: the threat from Sassanid Persia.

The success of this strategy was marked in December of 627 CE, when the Byzantine emperor Heraclius defeated the Sassanid dynasty's army at Nineveh. Heraclius took back Jerusalem and returned sacred relics that the Sassanids of Persia had plundered.

THE ECUMENICAL COUNCILS

A standard list of Ecumenical Councils, held under the protection of Constantinople, includes:

The Council of Nicea (325 CE)
The Council of Constantinople (381 CE)
The Council of Ephesus (431 CE)
The Council of Chalcedon (451 CE)
The Second Council of Constantinople (553 CE)
The Third Council of Constantinople (680–81 CE)
The Second Council of Nicea (787 CE)

But Heraclius overlooked the quarter from which a new threat emerged. In 630 CE Heraclius triumphantly returned the "Holy Cross" (wood on which Jesus had allegedly been crucified) to the Holy City, but he then saw his army, tens of thousands strong, defeated by the new Muslim forces at Yarmuk in August of 636 CE. Jerusalem fell two years later, and the Holy Cross had to be shipped off to Constantinople, while the "Holy Lance" that allegedly killed Jesus was removed to Antioch.

Muslim forces made dramatic incursions into Byzantine territory, aided both by flexible military campaigns and the heavy-handed policies that "new Rome" devised against alleged heretics. Some Christians preferred Muslim hegemony to acceding to the Orthodoxy (literally, "right opinion") imposed by Empire and Church acting in accord. But Constantinople survived and often thrived. In comparison with its might, pretensions from the West appeared trivial sometimes, and yet they could also prove trying.

On Christmas in 800 CE, Charlemagne, King of the Franks, had himself anointed "Emperor of the Romans" by the bishop of Rome. The ceremony enhanced the new emperor's stature, but it also solidified the growing reputation of the bishop, known locally as the *papa* or father of the city—in English, the "pope." Papacy and western claims to secular power grew together. But Constantinople rejected Charlemagne's claim, just as the Orthodox in the East refused to accept the move by Catholics in the West to change the wording of the Nicene Creed.

THE *FILIOQUE* CLAUSE

The phrase "and the Son" (*filioque* in Latin) was inserted into the last section of the Nicene Creed as recited in Latin churches. That addition meant that the Holy Spirit proceeded, not simply from the Father, but "from the Father and the Son." Although this change accorded with the theology of some of the great thinkers in Orthodoxy, Catholics made the change without the benefit of any ecumenical council of the Church. The principles for such a council had been established since Nicea: it was to be convened from bishops representing the whole inhabited land (the *oikoumene*) of the Church. Catholics' pretensions to act without such a worldwide council and in their own local language (Latin, rather than Greek) appeared arrogant in the East.

Despite such conflicts, successive Orthodox patriarchs (roughly equivalent to the popes in old Rome) welcomed the Western initiative during successive Crusades to win back the Holy Land. Even that pragmatic alliance proved disastrous. Financing campaigns became increasingly fraught, and Crusaders in 1204 responded to the demands of their backers in Venice by sacking the great city of Constantinople in order to raise money. Inadvertently helped by Hulagu Khan, who destroyed Baghdad in 1258, Constantinople won back some of its brilliance for more than two centuries, before succumbing to an Ottoman siege in 1453.

Whether in the cosmopolitan, troubled East or the agricultural, feudal West, violence as a threat or a reality governed the lands where Christianity held sway, both in the Roman Empire and beyond the Roman Empire. In the midst of invasions and conflicts, trumpeted victories and unexpected defeats, Christianity had to make its way in an environment of neither defeat nor triumph, but of uncertainty. As a result, Christians developed institutions on the basis of their common experience that made the Middle Ages a time of profound creativity.

ASKESIS

The Greek word *askesis* gives us the English adjective "ascetic," a term typically associated with practices in which a person deliberately deprives himself or herself of food, drink, sleep, sexual contact, and physical comfort. There is good reason for the association of the English term with deprivation, because many ascetic practices— especially during late Antiquity and the Middle Ages—were designed to promote hardship and even pain for the sake of advancement as a believer.

But ascetic practice and the theology that lies behind its disciplines cannot be understood by concentrating on what seems most alien to us and tracing how different it is from the values of our time. After all, ancient and medieval believers are not likely to have framed their lives in a way that would be immediately comprehensible to modern people, whether believers or not.

In its original meaning *askesis* does not refer to deprivation. Rather, it means "exercise" or "training." The root of ascetic practice in the Christian tradition is not self-abnegation for its own sake, but training on behalf of the most basic values of the faith.

Jesus commanded his followers, "If anyone wants to come after me, deny himself and take his cross and follow me!" (Mark 8:34). After this challenge, Mark's Gospel has Jesus add that, "Whoever wishes to save his own life will ruin it, but whoever will ruin his life for me and the message will save it" (Mark 8:35). That puts the same underlying wisdom in more general abstract terms. The Gospels often use repetition and paraphrase to convey Jesus' difficult teachings. In the case of these two sayings, a single truth, that the self needs to be lost for the self to be gained, is expressed as an imperative, to take up the cross, and as a proverb, about how to save one's life. These are teachings designed for meditation and incorporation into one's life, not just for quick learning or routine acceptance.

The purpose of Jesus' teaching was to focus on God's Kingdom as the chief ethical principle, so that self-interest was relegated as a motivation. His finding that the command to love God and to love one's neighbor were the foundation of the Law and the Prophets also serves to direct his disciples toward an aim that is not defined by their own desire.

Although a training or *askesis* is implicit in Jesus' ethics, the full impact of loyalty to his teaching rather than to the Roman Empire only became evident during the second century. During the period of persecution, Christians needed to decide whether or not to accede to the demand of magistrates that they should honor the gods of Rome and the genius of the emperor by burning incense and pouring out wine in front of one image or another. Some Gnostic Christians, following the advice of Paul that idols do not reflect anything real, believed they could follow these practices and remain faithful to Christ. Teachers such as Irenaeus decried their willingness to compromise in this way. He and Catholics like him insisted that God's sovereignty over the whole earth made it dishonest to behave as if actions in the social world did not matter. The opportunity to appeal to the conscience of persecutors demanded the avoidance of half-measures. To Irenaeus the willingness to suffer, to take up more than a metaphorical cross, was a requirement of faith.

Yet as Irenaeus recognized, the division between Catholics and Gnostics did not put them on different sides when it concerned the worst excesses of Roman persecution. Not content with forcing believers to worship the gods of Rome, some magistrates also insisted that they should curse Christ. Refusal to do so sometimes resulted in the torture and death of many Christians, Gnostics, and Catholics without discrimination.

Self-denial for the good of the faith under these circumstances meant steeling oneself for possible death. In order to promote this willingness to be a witness (the original sense of *martus* in Greek) to faith, Tertullian spoke of believers training themselves as soldiers train, to discipline themselves strategically to gain victory. The introduction of military rhetoric into the ethic of martyrdom occurred when Christians were still subject to persecution, and did not amount to any pretension to actual dominance within the Roman Empire.

The force of the rhetoric went far beyond the usual impact of a figure of speech. A noblewoman who was killed in the arena for her faith, Perpetua, describes a dream vision in which she sees her own body as a soldier's, trained and ready for combat. The fact that she had recently given birth makes the vision all the more stunning.

PERPETUA'S DREAM

The noblewoman Perpetua recorded her dream before her execution (*Martyrdom of Perpetua* 10) in Carthage early in the third century CE:

> And as I knew I had been condemned to the beasts, I was amazed that they did not send them out at me. And an Egyptian with a vicious look came out against me with his seconds to fight me. And handsome young men came out to me as seconds and supporters. And I was stripped naked and became a man, and my supporters began to rub me down with oil as they do before combat.

Because Perpetua had at this stage recently given birth, the application of masculine imagery is surreal. Despite her weakness, she is to do battle with a monstrous Egyptian, probably a symbol of the Roman Emperor Severus, who coiffed his hair and beard to look like the Egyptian god Serapis. No matter what his apparent power, the martyr's faith proves stronger.

Another martyr, a slave woman named Blandina, was, during the reign of Marcus Aurelius in the second century, subject to public torture by multiple means before she was killed. At one point, when she was naked and fastened to a stake, some people who attended the spectacle saw in her suffering a reflection of Jesus' crucifixion. Martyrdom became unwitting propaganda by the Romans against their own cruelty and for the Christians. The worse that could be said against the martyrs was that they were "obstinate" (as

Emperor Marcus Aurelius put it), while the cruelty of the executioners was vile by most standards.

With the growth of martyrdom the veneration of martyrs naturally emerged. They became the spiritual warriors of the new faith, who brought new converts to the Christ whose image they reflected. Already in the New Testament an ethic of the *imitatio Christi* (imitation of Christ) had emerged, and martyrs could claim to perfect their discipleship in the manner of their deaths.

Following Christ involved a life of transformation, so that the believers became more and more what 2 Peter 1:4 calls "participants of divine nature." Jesus' identity as Son of God, focused with increasing intensity by the teaching of the Trinity, promised those who were baptized and lived a committed life the prospect that they too would become God's children. Athanasius, a hero of Trinitarian orthodoxy, put the matter simply: "God became man that man might become God" (*On the Incarnation* 54:3).

Athanasius' saying is deliberately compressed, to the point of paradox. He wished to underline how Christ's coming in the flesh represented a restoration to humanity of the image and likeness of God in which people had been made primordially (see Genesis 1:26–27). Only God could overcome the estrangement of his children from him, and in Jesus God became fully human in order to rescue humanity from its self-indulgent idolatry.

The belief in the value of *askesis* was honed in the experience of the martyrs, but it applied to all who had been baptized. They, too, according to Paul, had been buried with Christ in his death and raised with him to newness of life (Romans 6:4). Yet in the case of the martyrs, Christians came to believe that human flesh had been divinized. Their remains (known as relics) brought those who came into contact with them into God's presence, with all its efficacy.

RELICS

Towards the end of his magisterial treatise, *The City of God* (c. 425 CE), Augustine provided an example of the power of relics that he said was amply documented:

> The miracle which was wrought at Milan when I was there and by which a blind man was restored to sight could come to the

knowledge of many; for not only is the city a large one, but also the emperor was there at the time, and the occurrence was witnessed by an immense concourse of people who had gathered to the bodies of the martyrs Protasius and Gervasius, which had long lain concealed and unknown, but were now made known to the bishop Ambrose in a dream and discovered by him. By virtue of these remains the darkness of that blind man was scattered, and he saw the light of day.

Relics of martyrs were signs of Christ's transformation, and the vanguard of a new creation. With loving detail, Augustine also described multiple miracles prompted by the presence of a portion of St Stephen's remains when they were transported to his own city of Hippo in North Africa.

North Africa was the site of a long established custom of what was called in Latin a *refrigerium* ("refreshment"), a meal held in a cemetery to honor the dead. In this practice, the departed were often held to join in the festivity, and early Christians took up this practice in the case of family members they had lost as well as martyrs. Early bishops did their best to curtail some excesses of the *refrigeria*, which could be more than raucous and easily turned to the veneration of gods worshipped long before the emergence of Christianity. But the similarity of this practice to the belief that Eucharist celebrated the presence of the risen Jesus was obvious.

As Christianity grew, relics of the saints came to be included in places of worship. A martyr's remains offered the prospect of healing and served as the focus of Eucharist. The saint was venerated as the patron of the church, and as churches multiplied, the relics of saints were subdivided. The holy flesh that the martyr produced became available to transform worshipers, so that they could become holy. The meaning of the Eucharist itself also developed, so that in the theology of Cyprian, the third-century bishop of Carthage, every single celebration of the Mass, as it came to be called in Latin, recollected the sacrifice of Jesus on the cross.

Christian teachers frequently made Isaac, who was nearly offered in sacrifice by his father, the patriarch Abraham, on Mount Moriah (Genesis 22), into a type of Christ on Golgotha. As a result, the offering of a Christian martyr could also be compared with that of Isaac or the ram that replaced Isaac in the Old Testament story. In the theology of the fourth century, by which time the Emperor Constantine had legalized Christianity, effectively making it the state religion of the Roman Empire, the martyr was not only a passive victim. *Roman soldiers* who fought the non-Catholic enemies of Rome were praised in hagiographies alongside those who had died under the persecutions of the previous centuries. The ancient Roman virtue of *devotio*, the willingness to be sacrificed in battle, was now applied to the Christian martyr, and the difference between the two became notional in what Augustine called the *res publica* of the faith.

These new martyrs were warriors as well as victims, and their blood dispelled the host of Satan even as their brawn shored up the Roman frontier. The fourth-century bishop and theologian, Gregory of Nyssa, speaks of weeping whenever he saw an icon of Isaac, and that is not surprising, because in Isaac's image shone the reflection of the past passion of Christ and the future sufferings of countless others in Christ's image and likeness. Gregory marks a key turn in the portrayal of Christ from the fourth century that continues until our time: the deeply emotional connection between the father and the son in Genesis 22 put their acts beyond reproach, and they were celebrated for their affections not only in sermons and hagiographies, but in plays, music, and poetry during the Middle Ages, the Renaissance, the Reformation, the Enlightenment, and the modern period.

But Gregory did not limit his concern to the restricted, and increasingly rare model of martyrs. Sainthood for him could be achieved by a life of active *askesis*, and he gave his own sister as an example (*Life of Macrina* 984–86; *c*.380). She conducted her life in a committed dedication to the removal of the desires of the flesh, to put her earthly passions to death in imitation of Christ.

THE PRAYER OF MACRINA

Gregory of Nyssa quotes Macrina on her deathbed as offering a model of devotion in her prayer to Christ (*Life of Macrina* 984–86):

Thou that didst break the flaming sword and didst restore to Paradise the man that was crucified with Thee and implored Thy mercies, remember me, too, in Thy kingdom; because I, too, was crucified with Thee, having nailed my flesh to the cross for fear of Thee, and of Thy judgments have I been afraid. Let not the terrible chasm separate me from Thy elect. Nor let the slanderer stand against me in the way; nor let my sin be found before Thy eyes, if in anything I have sinned in word or deed or thought, led astray by the weakness of our nature.

Gregory's fellow Trinitarian, Athanasius, developed the most influential biography of an ascetic in his *Life of Anthony*. An Egyptian like Athanasius, Anthony was a wealthy young man who took to heart Jesus' statement in the Gospel according to Matthew: "If you would be perfect, go, sell what you possess and give to the poor, and you will have treasure in heaven; and come, follow me" (Matthew 19:21). Perfection had long been held to be open to holy people, even before the coming of Christ. Origen had referred to "the saints who lived before the corporeal coming of Jesus and who had something more than the other faithful, so that they comprehended the mysteries of divinity" (*Commentary on John* 6.IV). The *logos* could teach even "before he became flesh" and could do no less afterward. Giving away his wealth, Anthony made his way into the wilderness of Egypt and lived there a spare existence centered on prayer and contemplation. Because he resided in the wilderness, for which the Greek term is *eremos*, Anthony became known as an *eremites*, or hermit.

In view of the lone existence of figures such as Anthony, the term "solitary" (*monakhos*) was also applied to them, the earliest "monks." In their ascetic practice, monks took on the austerities to live in the wilderness, concentrated on the tasks of prayer and meditation. Their practice brought about an increase in literacy and encouraged the use of the codex, papyrus sheets sewn to form a book, rather than the more cumbersome and fragile scroll. Contemplation of God assumed the shift of a person's focus from himself. The solitaries were overwhelmingly, although not exclusively, male; the capacity to make the decision to pursue such a life and to live unprotected assumed a degree of independence, confidence, and strength that were associated with men much more than with women.

In addition to the inevitable rigors that came with wilderness living, the solitaries also took on additional austerities. Reduced diet, exposure to the elements, the use of rough clothing, and the rejection of hygiene were all practices of wilderness contemplation. Some solitaries, called stylites, spent long periods on top of stone pillars (*stuloi* in Greek), sustained by the provisions that could be lifted to them, in order to shut out contact with others. Medieval Europe adapted the practice to fixing or anchoring a contemplative in a single place, so that the "anchorite" might be walled up in a corner or outbuilding of a church.

One of the most influential bishops of Rome (eventually called popes), Gregory the Great, compared the vocation of monastics with that of Mary Magdalene, whom he also identified with the unnamed penitent woman who washed Jesus' feet in Luke 7 (*Homily* 25, from 594 CE):

> We should reflect on Mary's attitude and the great love she felt for Christ; for though the disciples had left the tomb, she remained. She was still seeking the one she had not found, and while she sought she wept; burning with the fire of love, she longed for him who she thought had been taken away. And so it happened that the woman who stayed behind to seek Christ was the only one to see him. For perseverance is essential to any good deed, as the voice of truth tells us: Whoever perseveres to the end will be saved.

Gregory himself suffered ill health as a result of his prolonged periods of fasting, a common custom during the period.

Both in order to intensify their practice of contemplation and to mitigate practices that could be harmful when taken to extremes, monasticism developed along more social lines than the old term "solitary" would have suggested. Even heroic figures such as Anthony and Simeon Stylites were sought out for advice, counsel, and sometimes teaching during times of controversy within the Church. Over time, monks associated themselves and sometimes lived communally. Out of that, common or cenobitic monasticism emerged. The writings of John Cassian (c. 360–435), promoted the monastic way of life and inspired Benedict of Nursia (c.480–547), who developed a deeply influential rule of life centered on the vows of poverty, moderation, and obedience. Whether in orders such as Benedict's, in communal houses of cenobitic monks, or in the rugged life of solitaries, monasticism became a principal sign of and practice for union with God.

THE MONASTIC HOURS

The Benedictine hours set out a pattern of prayer and meditation during the course of the day. Each session might be called an office, and Catholic practice set out what was to be done at each office in a Breviary:

Matins (during the night)
Lauds (dawn)
Prime (on beginning activities)
Terce (mid-morning)
Sect (midday)
None (afternoon)
Vespers (evening)
Compline (before sleep).
Benedict's influence was profound in explaining and promoting the hours, but they represent a summary of monastic devotion as practiced very widely in Christendom.

ATONEMENT

The word "atonement" in English was a term made up from its elements: "at," "one," "ment." The English noun and its related verb ("atone") were used from the fourteenth century on to speak of reconciliation between people, but over time their theological application predominated. Paul described God as reconciling the world to himself through Christ, and therefore giving believers the task of reconciliation (2 Corinthians 5:19). Atonement refers to the divine and human task of reconciliation with one another.

From the time of Paul, atonement has been conceived along cosmic as well as personal lines. In this analysis, Christ is the "last Adam." While the first, primordial Adam was a living being, Jesus became an eschatological life-giving spirit (1 Corinthians 15:45). This theology caused early thinkers to conceive of Jesus as completing the epic of human destiny, from Eden to heaven. For Irenaeus in the Latin West, the idea was expressed as Christ's "recapitulation" (*recapitulatio*) of the whole potential of humanity, while for Origen in the Greek East, the term "restoration" (*apokatastasis*) captured the sense of Christ's atonement. In either case, the focus was on the summing up of human experience by means of Jesus' life, death, resurrection, and ascension.

Irenaeus began with a pragmatic view of human nature. People were made in the image and likeness of God (Genesis 1:26–27), but the divine likeness had been tarnished, even occluded, by sin. The divine image nonetheless remained. What was necessary for atonement, then, was to bring back the moral power to act in accordance with God's will. Irenaeus' background helps to explain his theology. He was not a convert to Christianity, but a product of Christian culture in Asia Minor, in which the close proximity of God's Spirit was an axiom. Irenaeus was nurtured in a milieu which anticipated the immediate fulfillment of biblical promises in Christ, and his theory of recapitulation was not intended as an historical survey, but as an answer to the single question: How is it that faith in Jesus Christ will ultimately transform humanity?

This theory elevated the flesh to the realm of what would be saved, and it was Irenaeus who inspired Athanasius' theology. He said before Athanasius, "God became man that man might become divine" (*Against Heresies* 3.10.2; 3.19.1; 4.33.4, 11). Because Irenaeus rooted his analysis in people as creatures of flesh, he articulated a hope in the sanctification of flesh that was symmetrical with his conception of primordial sin in the flesh. His conviction that human beings were subject to sin and yet susceptible to transformation, so as to turn the inheritance of Adam into the glory of Christ, became a staple of early Christian preaching.

For Irenaeus, as for the Epistle to the Hebrews and Justin Martyr, the Incarnation of Christ told the real meaning of Israel's Scriptures outside the order of what we call real time. Chronology did not have any theological significance for thinkers who believed the Son of God was eternal.

Since recapitulation, like typology, is a theory of salvation rather than an historical argument, Irenaeus is able to make statements about Jesus without recourse to information about him, openly contradicting a literal reading of the Gospels. Because Jesus recapitulates or sums up our humanity in his flesh, Irenaeus holds he must have died around the age of fifty, the supposed time of complete human maturity (*Against Heresies* 2.22.1–6). The only reference in the New Testament to Jesus' age comes in the Gospel according to Luke, where he "began to be about thirty" (Luke 3:23). Although that statement is vague, only abstract speculation can turn Jesus' age at his death into fifty.

Irenaeus' view of salvation involved the flesh from its beginning in types, in its recapitulation in the case of Jesus, and in its fulfillment in paradise. Gnostic theology, by contrast, referred to flesh as ancillary, an accident in the overall unfolding of spiritual essence.

The procedure of thinking on the basis of God's nature and relating that to human nature, pioneered in the Epistle to the Hebrews and pursued by Irenaeus, is perhaps best instanced by Origen of Alexandria. Born in 185 CE, Origen knew the consequences that faith could endure in the Roman world: His father died in the persecution under the Roman emperor Septimus Severus in 202 CE. Origen accepted the sort of renunciation demanded of apostles in the Gospels, putting aside his possessions to develop what Christians of the time called the philosophical life, a life consistent with the wisdom of the Gospels (see Eusebius, *History of the Church* 6.3). His learning resulted in his appointment to the catechetical school in Alexandria.

Eusebius also reports that Origen castrated himself (*History of the Church* 6.8), inspired by Jesus' teaching in Matthew 19:12, but it seems likely he is repeating a calumny by Demetrios, bishop of Alexandria, who objected to Origen's ordination by the bishops of Jerusalem and Caesarea. Origen moved from Alexandria to Caesarea in Palestine, to some extent as a result of a bitter dispute with Demetrios, his episcopal nemesis. During the persecution of the emperor Decius (250 CE) Origen was tortured, and he died of consequent ill health in 254 CE.

Origen was the most powerful Christian thinker of his time. He opened the way in the comparative study of texts of the Old Testament, while his commentaries and sermons illustrate the development of a conscious method of interpretation. His most characteristic work, *On First Principles*, is the earliest comprehensive

Christian philosophy extant. It offers a systematic account of God, the world, free will, and Scripture. His *Against Celsus* is a classic work of apologetics, and his contribution to the theory and practice of prayer (represented in the classic source of meditation edited by Basil the Great during the fourth century, the *Philokalia*) is unparalleled. Throughout, Origen remains a creative and challenging thinker. Condemned by later councils of the Church for his daring assertion that even fallen angels could theoretically one day repent and be saved (see *Apology* I.6), Origen stands as the most controversial theologian in the Christian tradition.

Unlike Irenaeus, Origen insisted upon the transformation of existence from earth to heaven as a radical spiritualization of the human body. The line of demarcation between millennial expectations of eschatology (such as Justin's and Irenaeus') and spiritual expectations of eschatology (such as Paul's and Origen's) is quite clear in classical Christianity, and the difference has not been resolved to this day.

The aim of true interpretation according to Origen was to find the allegorical or spiritual meaning that provides insight into the restoration (*apokatastasis*) of all things in Christ, a transformation that can only occur outside the terms and conditions of this world. Any limitation to the realm of literal history was for Origen a dangerous self-deception.

The difference between Irenaeus and Origen is instructive on several levels. They both invested what happened to Jesus in the flesh with profound meaning, but in different ways. In Irenaeus' millennial perspective, what happened in the case of one person of flesh has consequence for all people of flesh, and vice versa. According to Origen's philosophical mode of thought, Jesus' flesh is important as the occasion to reveal the divine nature of the spiritual body, a reality that only the restoration of all things will manifest fully.

The difference between the *recapitulatio* of Irenaeus and the *apokatastasis* of Origen is more than a matter of nomenclature. It also reflects the dividing line between millennial and philosophical views of eschatological transformation and distinctive assessments of the value of the flesh. Flesh is the medium of revelation in Irenaeus, while it is more loosely related to revelation in Origen. Although both views recognize the flesh of Jesus and believers' flesh as consequential, they disagree on how the promise of humanity is realized. For

Irenaeus, flesh is to become eternal in the millennial rule of the saints promised in Revelation 20:4. For Origen, thinking more along the lines of Paul (1 Corinthians 15:42–49) than of the Revelation, flesh is to be transformed into the medium of God's Spirit.

The means by which people could attach themselves to this recapitulation or restoration became a burning question for Origen. He associated Christ with the lamb of Passover, the scapegoat of the Day of Atonement, and the ram discovered by Abraham on Moriah, all within the typology of Isaac. Origen produced a rich and at the same time a lucid expression of the eternal sacrifice that Christ offered.

The understanding of Christ's death as a sacrifice goes back to the New Testament. According to the logic of the ancient world, a life offered in sacrifice produced divine enjoyment, which enhanced the life of the sacrificing community. In Exodus, for example, Israelites are commanded to offer the firstborn males of all domestic animals in commemorations of their liberation of Egypt, but to redeem every firstborn son (Exodus 13:11–16). Each is "redeemed" by the offering of an animal. A person could be neither sacrificed nor killed, so that firstborn human males needed to be redeemed. "Redemption" meant more than merely paying money in the Hebrew Bible, although payment also was sometimes involved.

The Torah presents various conceptions of redemption. By a priestly reckoning, the life of each Levite belonged to God (Numbers 3:44–51), and so redeemed the life of an Israelite firstborn son. In this case, each Levite is literally a living sacrifice. Confronted with the problem of firstborn sons over and above the number of Levites, the same passage demands payment in "the shekel of the sanctuary." When the question of payment does arise, the transaction in money or kind is not the aim of sacrifice, but deals with cases in which sacrifice cannot be performed in the classic manner. It would be truer to say that in the Scriptures of Israel commercial exchange was the substitute for sacrifice than the reverse.

By the time of Origen, however, that equation had been turned backwards. For centuries, Jews had been mocking Greco-Roman sacrifices as vain attempts to bribe the gods, Hellenistic philosophers had ridiculed the superstitious attempts of their contemporaries to curry divine favor with gifts from the human world, and Christians had been attacking both Jews and Greeks as literalists, idolaters—and more often than not, as both.

This deep-seated attitude in Christian sensibility, which made ritual as such appear contemptible, left theologians of the Church bereft of means to appreciate why the Israelites had ever conceived of God as enjoying sacrifice in the first place. The divine pleasure that resulted in God deciding not to flood the earth again after Noah's offering (Genesis 8:20–22), to preserve Jerusalem after David's offering (2 Samuel 24:17–25), as well as to save Isaac's life from Abraham's knife (Genesis 22:1–18), is not a part of Origen's sacrificial equation.

Once Christian thought had conceived of Christ as replacing sacrifice, as it had done since the Epistle to the Hebrews, it had difficulty explaining why God would really be pleased with sacrifice in any case. Every ritual operation seemed to have resulted from Jewish misunderstanding and literalism, while the spiritual meaning of the Israelite Scriptures pointed to Christ's sacrifice alone. From the time of the Epistle to the Hebrews, and through *The Epistle of Barnabas*, as well as the writings of Justin Martyr, Irenaeus, and Origen, this approach to the whole question of sacrifice became more and more entrenched. That ancient Christian attitude helps explain why today, many people assume that a devotion to "ritual" rather than to "spirituality" is a sign of religious immaturity and why Judaism is often dismissed as a throwback form of faith.

Because Origen deliberately replaced anything approaching an historical evaluation of texts with his typological approach, focused on eternity rather than happenstance, he was in no position to recover the underlying purpose of sacrifice in Israel's Scriptures. Indeed, he thought the aim of theology was to transcend any such earlier belief with faith in Christ. The stage was set for sacrificial offering to be mistaken as a commercial transaction, ironically with the justification that this corresponded to the spiritual meaning of Scripture.

It did not help that, in Greek, a single word, *lutron*, might mean "redemption," "rescue," or "ransom." Linguistic imprecision has long influenced the translation of a saying of Jesus (Mark 10:45): "For even the son of man did not come to be served, but to serve, and to give his life, a *lutron* for many." The sacrificial sense of these words is lost in the image of a commercial transaction by commentators who are out of touch with the Semitic environment in which Jesus taught, where the Aramaic word *purqana'*, which the term *lutron* represents, clearly means "redemption" rather than "ransom."

Origen believed that sacrifice was so much a matter of the mistaken past that, when it came to explaining the efficacy of Jesus' sacrificial death, only the commercial model of a payment made sense to him. On that model, it seemed to him evident that in the crucifixion God handed over his own Son. He gave what Abraham had finally not been required to give in Genesis 22. From this model it seemed clear that the payment had been made to Satan, the custodian of sin's power.

By portraying that sacrifice as a ransom paid to the devil, Origen also explained the eternal value of that sacrifice: In principle, every sin ever committed, or ever to be committed, had been compensated for by the crucifixion, because after the payment of Jesus' life, the devil could expect no further recompense. In framing this theology of atonement by Christ's blood, which compensated for the sins of humanity as a whole, past and present, Origen was extending a line of thought that also promoted even more radical applications of the typology of Isaac.

Cyril of Alexandria in the fifth century signals a determinative shift in the understanding of Christ's death, which came to light fully during the Middle Ages, and continues to shape how, in the modern period, readers see God himself as the hidden hand behind both the story of Abraham and Isaac and Jesus' crucifixion. In making the crucifixion God's active desire, Cyril posed a stark contrast between the sacrifice that *God* (rather than Satan) wants and the Old Testament scene. When Isaac, "having been placed on the wood, is stolen away from death and suffering," Isaac and his Jewish progeny (*Pascal Homilies* 5) cheated God of what he most desired. On this reading, the Old Testament "type" was so faulty, it effectively inverted the reality that Christ accomplished. Despite the popular teaching, defended on Origen's authority, that the devil accepted Jesus' death as a ransom, the view steadily gained ground that violence for the sake of God, including the death of his own Son, fulfilled the Father's pleasure.

Cyril's God *wanted* human sacrifice, in Isaac's time, in Christ's—and beyond. The Old Testament and the Jews had denied God what he wanted most, Christ had accomplished God's will, and it was left to Christians to pursue Christ's sacrificial action to its logical conclusion. Christian mobs rioted against pagans in Alexandria in 415 CE, encouraged by Cyril, the local bishop; they dragged the Neo-Platonist philosopher Hypatia from her chariot, stripped and flayed her—and then burned her alive.

THE SON'S DEATH AS A SACRIFICE TO THE FATHER

Alongside his militant campaign of religious cleansing in Alexandria, Cyril developed distinctive, influential ideas in his interpretation of both Christ's death and Abraham's offering. When it concerns a Christological reading of Genesis 22, Cyril concludes that "the child being led to the sacrifice by his father indicates through symbol and outline that neither human strength nor the greed of the conspirator led our Lord Jesus Christ to the cross, but the desire of the Father." This turns around Origen's theory of Christ's death as a ransom paid to the devil. Now it is *God's* active desire, not Satan's, which stands behind the action.

Even as Origen's theory of Christ's death as a ransom paid to the devil was increasingly replaced by Cyril's view of the crucifixion as payment to God, literal payment grew as a method of righting wrongs in Medieval Europe. This was an inheritance of customs of Europe before the Roman conquest that later passed into Common Law. Whether for divine forgiveness or to assuage a desire for vengeance, paying in money or in kind for crimes, even murder (for which *weregild*, "man-coin," was demanded), became widespread. As a method of justice, the approach of enforceable recompense clearly had advantages, offering benefits to victims of crime and inflicting palpable losses on offenders without the enormous social costs associated with incarceration and execution. Because arrangements in society were projected onto humanity's relationship to God during the Middle Ages, often with little reflection, sins also came to be compensated by specific amounts, which were duly published in penitential manuals.

Amounts paid to compensate for sin could obviously not be thought of as being paid to the devil, as in Origen's theory of the ransom. Even the thought of compensating God for sin required explanations of gymnastic proportions; making the concept work with Satan seemed hopeless. So Anselm, the archbishop of Canterbury who died in 1109, converted Cyril of Alexandria's suggestion into a fully renovated ransom theory and deliberately refuted Origen. In Anselm's analysis, it must be God who receives the recompense for human sin, with Christ's death the gift of a blameless and noble life in recompense for the guilt of others. Among educated readers today, Søren Kierkegaard has made Anselm's interpretation canonical, while Christian Fundamentalists have made his ransom theory a *requirement* of belief, apart from which salvation is impossible.

Although the devil had been banished by Anselm's scheme, a new twist was introduced into the logic of atonement that proved diabolical. Blood became precious, either as the innocent payment one might offer in imitation of the sacrifice or Christ, or as the punishment that virtuous people could rightly inflict on evildoers. By the faithful rituals of sacraments that included acts of penance and related practices, believers understood that their actions could be part of the realization of atonement when directed by the orthodoxy of their creeds.

On this understanding, there was a crucial distinction between mortal sins, which required eternal punishment, and venial sins, which might be purged by temporal means. Manuals of penitence set out what a sinner must do to deal with his or her error, and—when the means of this world were insufficient—the doctrine of purgatory permitted an interval after death, but before definitive judgment, for God to work out his justice.

SEVEN DEADLY SINS, PURGATORY, AND INDULGENCE

In 590 CE Pope Gregory I, on the basis of a long tradition, conceived of the principal sins that can lead to damnation as lust, gluttony, greed, sloth, wrath, envy, and pride.

For instances in which sins did not lead to damnation, but nonetheless damaged a relationship of grace with God, purgatory was conceived of as a place of cleansing. During the third century, Origen believed that after death all souls needed to be educated in the vision of God. But by the Middle Ages, the idea of education had been replaced by the notion of the necessary punishment for sin. This was linked to the belief that acts of piety, for one's own benefit or on behalf of a dead loved one, might reduce the duration of cleansing or punishment in purgatory. In 1095, Pope Urban II preached the First Crusade, and promised indulgence to those who took part, treating their combat as a combination of penance and pilgrimage.

Atonement on this understanding was an ethical structure that included this world and the next in tight coordination with ritual means of forgiveness. Sacraments now included not only Eucharist and Baptism, but also penance. In fact, the West saw the rite as of such importance that the Fourth Lateran Council of 1215 required confession and penance of all Catholics as a condition of receiving communion. The same council also required celibacy of all clergy and put them in a condition of monastic obedience to the Pope. Atonement became the hierarchical and sacramental aim of the entire system of belief.

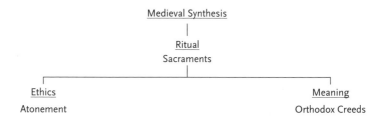

Although penance and a sense of payment animated this system, the earlier view, which saw divine forgiveness in non-commercial terms, did not pass away. In the East, the "Jesus Prayer" summed up the contemplative practice that connected monastics and lay people alike. By praying, "Lord Jesus Christ, Son of God, Savior, have mercy on me, a sinner," practitioners became aware of God's compassion in a way that suffused their daily activities. Devotion, rather than payment, became their rule of life. In the West, the doctrine of Transubstantiation made Eucharist a continuing, miraculous presence that no human effort could have produced.

TRANSUBSTANTIATION

Thomas Aquinas (1225–74) taught that, in the Eucharist, the "accidents," or physical composition, of bread and wine did not change, but their "substance"—their intellectual immaterial reality—became the body and blood of Christ. This was his teaching of "transubstantiation," a philosophical doctrine emblematic of Thomas's capacity to link empirical observation in the classical tradition with the Platonist teachings of the church that conceived of "substance" in ideal terms.

NEARNESS TO CHRIST, PILGRIMAGE, AND HOLY WAR

By the Middle Ages, an entire calendar enabled believers to mark out their time on earth in terms of their practice of Christianity. For all its complexity, the Christian calendar is oriented by three great moments: Easter, Pentecost, and what is best termed, in the Orthodox tradition, Epiphany. Easter and Pentecost are obvious in their centrality. Reference to Epiphany, which actually commences the tripartite cycle, probably puzzles some readers, who think of Christmas as the initial festival of the year. As is widely agreed, however, Christmas is a fourth-century refinement of a festival much broader in significance, a celebration of the Incarnation of God in Christ, not only of Jesus' birth, the ancient Epiphany. The term Epiphany itself means "manifestation," and refers to Christ's manifestation of God on earth; in fact, Epiphany is sometimes called "Theophany" by ancient writers.

The underlying function of this entire complex is to present the eternal action of God in Christ. In all that is recollected of the acts and events concerning Christ, history and eternity meet during the yearly calendar. The sense of meeting eternity in a time out of time is strengthened by the practice of regular worship on Sundays. Sunday, the first day of the week, is also called the eighth day in the Christian tradition, in order to signal that, after a completed week, a week such as the one in which God created the world, a new creation commences with the resurrection of Christ.

Every Sunday is a feast of the resurrection. Its time is calculated from sundown on the Sabbath, and it proceeds through the depths of the night when Christ was known to be dead and dawns with the power of new and unanticipated life. Historically, we may infer that the timing of the Christian Eucharist permitted Christian Jews both to keep Sabbath and to worship Christ, but at base Sunday signals a fresh creative act of God in raising Jesus. Christians meet then to join themselves to that divine creativity, in a time that takes them out of ordinary time and into an experience of eternity.

For just this reason, Easter is always celebrated on a Sunday. The ancient connection to the Paschal season is retained (and Paschal language is employed to speak of Jesus' death and resurrection), but what is celebrated is the resurrection, not Israel's liberation from Egypt as such. Passover is computed by beginning with the first new moon after the spring equinox and counting fourteen days (to the full moon). Easter is computed by taking the Sunday following the full moon after the equinox. Because the Orthodox Church has never accepted the Gregorian reform of the calendar (which came long after East and West went their separate ways in 1582), its Easter and the West's do not match up. So the two Easters and Passover are always within reach of another and yet doggedly out of phase.

The Paschal season became the normative period for the final instruction and preparation of catechumens (those being instructed) for baptism. As a result, a time of fasting before Easter was observed, although the season now called Lent only emerged slowly and was kept for various lengths of time. Fasting (especially on Wednesdays and Fridays, in deliberate distinction from Jewish fasts on Tuesdays and Thursdays) was a characteristic feature of early Christian devotion from the second century. Its aim was to focus prayer and also to prepare the believer for the spiritual celebration that was to come on Sunday. During Lent, an emphasis on repentance (following the theme of John's baptism) was also very strong.

Because Easter is always on a Sunday, Christian Pentecost—seven weeks (or fifty days) later—also falls on a Sunday. Its great theme of the endowment of Spirit which comes from the risen Christ obviously links it inextricably with Easter, which makes any sense of the wheat harvest or even the giving of the law (as in Jewish *Shavuoth*) residual. Just as the Christian Paschal Mysteries are a signal development, not a repetition of Passover, so Pentecost can be related typologically to the Judaic feast, although a radically different character also needs to be acknowledged. But celebrations of the Holy Spirit in Christianity have often occurred during the summer months in the northern hemisphere, and there are many examples of informal local festivals at that time of the year.

Just as Christianity could relate typologically to Judaism in its Easter and its Pentecost, understanding Christ as the hidden reality within the ancient types of Exodus and Torah, so Christians could absorb the symbols, images, and festivals of other cultures as types. That absorption has fed the variety of Christian theology and contributed signally to what is today a very complex calendar that has grown out of the Julian model of the Roman Empire and its eventual revision. For the most part, those developments (such as the much commented upon day of St. Valentine) do not concern us here. But when it comes to Epiphany, we face the stark fact of that absorption at an extremely early period.

There is good evidence to support the analysis that Epiphany has been kept from the time of the second century, and its emergence is even signaled in the Gospel according to John (*c.*100 CE). January 6 had been an ancient Egyptian feast of light, kept at what was thought to be the time of the winter solstice. This celebration was also associated with the god Dionysus and his mythic capacity to turn water into wine. Christians at that time kept that day as the dawn of the light into the world, especially when Jesus was baptized. John's Gospel—in its references to light, baptism, and Jesus' visit to Cana (when water became wine) in its opening section (John 1:1–2:11)—marks the emergence of the Christian Epiphany.

Although believers during the Middle Ages could draw near to God while remaining in place, pilgrimage became the typical mark of piety and a powerful vehicle of penance. The journey to visit the relics of a saint, near or far, meant proximity to holiness and the promise of a new beginning in the life of salvation. By this time, Origen's view of the afterlife as a time of preparation leading to heaven crystallized in the doctrine of purgatory, a place of cleansing (rather than the eternal punishment of Hell) that might endure many thousands of years for a given person. Pilgrimage offered to shorten that time, and the papacy gave indulgences, remissions from purgatory for stated times, in exchange for pilgrimage and other acts of piety.

Pope Urban II, preaching the Crusade in many places in France between 1095 and his death in 1099, made unmistakable his recourse to the view that bloodshed purifies the believer's constitutional violence and pleases God. He called for warriors who would literally bear the cross on their chests, celebrating their release from sin as they went into battle. Part of his argument was that a good war against a common foe would at last resolve the problem of internecine squabbles in Medieval Europe.

PREACHING THE CRUSADES

There is a problem of sources in documenting what Pope Urban II said to support his call for Crusades, as in the case of many events during the "Dark Ages," as historians used to call the period. But it seems clear from the chronicle of Fulcher of Chartres that his argument was based on the appeal for the remission of sins:

> Remission of sins will be granted for those going there, if they end a shackled life either on land, in crossing the sea, or in struggling against the heathen. I, being vested with that gift from God, grant this to those who go. Let those who are accustomed to wage private wars wastefully even against believers go forth against the infidels in a battle worthy to be undertaken now and to be finished in victory.

Urban grounded his argument for why Crusaders should go forth to battle with an assessment of their present sinful condition at home. Somehow, violence in Europe had to be addressed, and because violence was believed to be an inescapable part of the human condition, directing it far from Europe's doorstep seemed the best option. Urban believed that fractious warriors at home could be transformed in the crucible of holy war.

By means of both the blood they shed and the blood they offered, the Crusaders became living sacrifices in Pope Urban's appeal:

> Everyone who has decided to make his holy pilgrimage and has made a promise to God and has vowed that he will pour himself out to him as a living, holy, and pleasing sacrifice must bear the sign of the Lord's cross on his front or breast. Anyone who after fulfilling his vow wishes to return must put the sign on his back between his shoulder blades.

Urban made an explicit connection between the Crusaders and the Maccabees before them, directly comparing Maccabean combat "for rituals and the Temple" with the new struggle for the *patria*, the "fatherland." It is often observed that the Crusades combined zeal for pilgrimage and penitence with assertions of national and papal power. Those observations are valid, but the extraordinary popular energy unleashed by the Crusades has puzzled historians, chiefly because their sacrificial dimension has not been factored in.

The joy and energy of the Crusades were such that popular response to Urban's call wildly exceeded expectations, and Crusaders became notoriously difficult to control. After all, Urban promised a reward for the present as well as the future. As the twelfth-century historian Orderic Vitalis said of Urban: "He absolved all the penitent from all their sins from the hour they took the Lord's cross and he lovingly released them from all hardships, whether fasting or other mortification of the flesh." Crusading was a license, not only to kill, but also to eat one's fill, in the assurance one was absolved in advance from the sins of murder and greed.

Battle took the place of ordinary penance and the considerable disciplines usually preceded forgiveness. In the First Crusade alone, between 60,000 and 100,000 people—men, women, and children—answered the call, many of them totally untrained and served up for slaughter in what is modern Turkey.

IMAGES OF THE INFIDEL

Urban had also dramatized the depravity of the infidels during his famous speaking tour:

> These men have destroyed the altars polluted by their foul practices. They have circumcised the Christians, either spreading the blood from the circumcisions on the altars or pouring it into the baptismal fonts. And they cut open the navels of those whom they choose to torment with loathsome death, tear out their most vital organs and tie them to a stake, drag them around, and flog them, before killing them as they lie prone on the ground with all their entrails out. What shall I say of the appalling violation of women?

Retribution and pilgrimage were combined in the Crusades, but the aim was salvation. Violence had been baptized as the activist's route to heaven. Because this militant zeal targeted those who rejected faith in Christ, many Crusaders took out the full extremity of their initial enthusiasm on Jews in their own communities before they left for the Holy Land or on Jews who lay along their path to Jerusalem. Although this might seem a gross confusion, the Crusaders were convinced of the family resemblance among all infidels. Peter the Venerable, a popular leader and a learned abbot who had the Qur'an translated into Latin in order to refute it, came to the conclusion in 1146 that God rejects "the Jews like the hateful Cain, the Muslims like the worshippers of Baal." Pogroms by Crusaders began as early as 1095 in Rouen and continued into the Rhineland. Campaigns against defenseless Jews punctuated the violent progress of the Crusades, finally far exceeding the Crusades themselves in duration, virulence, and body count.

Describing the taking of the Temple Mount by the Crusaders in 1099 CE, Raymond d'Aguilers wrote that the blood on the Temple Mount reached up to the bridles of the Crusaders' horses as they slaughtered their Muslim enemies. That picture is literally apocalyptic, drawn from the book of the Revelation (14:20), but it is also bathed in the conviction that blood cleanses the guilty. A monk and chronicler of the time, Guibert of Nogent, appreciated and repeated Urban's aim, saying, "God has instituted in our time holy wars, so that the order of knights and the crowd running in their wake, who, following the example of ancient pagans, have been engaged in slaughtering one another, might find a new way of gaining salvation."

Experience proved otherwise. Crusaders' violence did not free the Holy Land over the long run; enhanced weaponry only exacerbated Europe's internecine wars; even Constantinople, which had welcomed the project of the Crusades, was left smoking in the Crusaders' wake. The delicate task of finding policies that would control the forces unleashed by the Crusades was one of many revisions that the theology of the Middle Ages required.

Yet an enduring strength of the medieval church resided in its capacity to form and shape institutions that proved resilient. Even as the structures of Rome were attenuated by territorial expansion, repeated invasions, and official corruption, monasteries took over the functions of education and poor relief that had once been political prerogatives. Hospitals emerged for the care of pilgrims throughout Christendom. By the twelfth century, universities emerged out of the teaching of monks in cities, while the cities themselves were enriched by the Crusades. Special needs of teaching at an advanced level and mounting theological arguments against opponents led to the foundation of the Order of Preachers by St. Dominic.

Dominic's order found its influence grow exponentially in the combat with the Cathars, a Christian group in the south of France that sought what they called a way of perfection. They believed that even Jesus was subject to minor sins, but that he showed the way for salvation to all, regardless of station. Pope Innocent III was outraged by the Cathar teaching that Mary Magdalene was Jesus' concubine, although his vehemence may have had more to do with the Cathars' denial of papal authority and refusal to pay tithes to the

Church than with their peculiar teaching about Jesus and Mary. Innocent declared a crusade against the Cathars in 1209, displaying just how widely the concept might be applied. The result has been called the first European genocide.

On July 22, 1209 crusaders dispatched by the pope torched the town of Béziers, killing both the Cathars who had fled there and the Roman Catholic population that had refused to give them up. Some 15,000 people died that day. One pious chronicler rejoiced, "that these disgusting dogs were taken and massacred during the feast of the one that they had insulted."

But what of the innocent? As the papal legate, Arnaud–Amaury, ordered the execution, he was asked how the Crusaders would know Cathars from Catholics. He replied: "Kill them all! The Lord will know his own." That initiated a royal tradition of killing Cathars that successfully made the transition to killing Protestants after the Reformation and all but eradicated both groups in France.

In the person of Thomas Aquinas, however, the same Dominican order that had proved instrumental in the crusade against the Cathars changed the conception of warfare. In this case, as in others, medieval theology proved its capacity to think beyond the boundaries it had initially set for itself.

CAN WAR BE JUST?

Thomas Aquinas doubted whether war could be just. His concern was to mitigate the sin inherent in war. His teaching was deliberately unoriginal, a scholastic summary of previous views, crystallized for what he recognized as the particular circumstances of his time. He endorsed the extension of the papal indulgence to the Crusades on the grounds that they met with the necessary conditions:

> For an indulgence to benefit anyone, however, three things are required. First, a cause that appertains to the honor of God, or for the necessity or utility of the church. Secondly, authority in him who grants it: the pope principally, others insofar as they receive either ordinary or commissioned, that is, delegated,

power from him. Thirdly, it is required that the one who wishes
to receive the indulgence should be in the state of charity.

But this argument is only possible because Thomas
takes the Crusades as a special case, for the honor of God.
Notably, the Crusades would not meet his strictures on
when war might be fought under unusual circumstances.

Thomas quotes Augustine extensively in posing the
question of whether it is always sinful to wage war. In
elucidating the consideration that competent authority
should wage war, he particularly argues against private war.
Because that was a besetting problem in his time (which
the Crusades had not resolved), he also stresses that war
must be a response to a genuine evil or fault and that the
intention of going to war should be in the ultimate interests
of peace. The last condition is so extensively discussed that
Thomas in effect introduces a fourth condition: that peace
should be the anticipated outcome of action and that this
purpose should be expressed even during the conduct of
war, and specifically towards one's enemy.

Thomas's strictures are such that not only private warfare but even the actual conduct of the Crusades is implicitly put in the category of sin. But the theoretical purity of
the Crusades permitted war to be promoted, not only
condoned, by teachers after Thomas.

SUMMARY

In this chapter we have seen that:

- *Askesis* became the engine of the formation of monasteries
  as well as of personal discipline during the Middle Ages.
- Consequently, the interior life as well as institutions
  became centers of devotion.
- Martyrdom was a standard of devotion long after the
  period of Roman persecution had ended.
- The result was, however, to insist upon the vital importance
  of atonement.

- During this period atonement was articulated in terms of Christ's sacrifice to the Father, although other less formal means included the Jesus Prayer and the teaching of Transubstantiation.
- The sacrificial model, however, fed the theory and practice of the Crusades during the Middle Ages.
- Medieval theology, nevertheless, also encouraged the growth of institutions which gradually reformed Christian teaching in regard to war.

FURTHER READING

Asbridge, Thomas (2004) *The First Crusade. A New History* (Oxford: Oxford University Press).

Bartlett, Robert (ed.) (2001) *Medieval Panorama* (Los Angeles: J. Paul Getty Museum).

Brown, Peter (1996) *The Rise of Western Christendom. Triumph and Diversity, 200–1000 AD* (Cambridge: Blackwell).

Bynum, Caroline Walker (1995) *The Resurrection of the Body in Western Christianity, 200–1336* (New York: Columbia University Press).

Chilton, Bruce (2008) *Abraham's Curse. Child Sacrifice in the Legacies of the West* (New York: Doubleday).

McGinn, Bernard (1998) *Visions of the End. Apocalyptic Traditions in the Middle Ages* (New York: Columbia University Press).

Newman, Barbara (ed.) (1998) *Voice of the Living Light. Hildegard of Bingen and her World* (Berkeley, CA: University of California Press).

4

REFORMATION AND ENLIGHTENMENT BASICS
FAITH IN THE MIDST OF DISPUTE

The Reformation exerted a revolutionary impact on Europe during the sixteenth century, but its roots lie in forces that began to show their power during the Middle Ages. The signature concern of Martin Luther, those associated with him, and even his most articulate opponents was the nature and the importance of faith. In particular, faith during the Reformation came to be seen as a standard higher than that of authority within the Church. But with the teaching of St. Francis of Assisi, Medieval Europe had already experienced such a claim and its revolutionary consequences.

ST. FRANCIS

Born into a wealthy family in 1182, Francis of Assisi committed himself to a life of poverty over the objections of his father. He went on to found the Order of the Friars Minor, which he saw as fulfilling the command Jesus gave his apostles to preach God's Kingdom freely, without the resources of money, extra clothing, or even sandals (Matthew 10:7–10). Pope Innocent III approved the order in 1210, and an order of women was added under Clare of Assisi. Owing to his wish to keep the rule of his followers in accord with the gospel alone in their vows of obedience, poverty, and chastity, Francis encountered a great deal of resistance over time from the curia, the court of the papacy. He lived in seclusion toward the end of his life, and before his death in 1226, reliable informants say that he received the stigmata, the marks of Christ's wounds on his own body.

Francis lived during the time of the troubadours, and his "Canticle of the Sun," largely a paraphrase of Psalm 148, remains a monument to his spirituality:

> Be praised, my Lord, through all Your creatures, especially through my lord Brother Sun, who brings the day; and You give light through him. And he is beautiful and radiant in all his splendor! Of You, Most High, he bears the likeness.
>
> Be praised, my Lord, through Sister Moon and the stars; in the heavens You have made them bright, precious, and beautiful.
>
> Be praised, my Lord, through Brothers Wind and Air, and clouds and storms, and all the weather, through which You give Your creatures sustenance.
>
> Be praised, my Lord, through Sister Water; she is very useful, and humble, and precious, and pure.
>
> Be praised, my Lord, through Brother Fire, through whom You brighten the night. He is beautiful and cheerful, and powerful and strong.
>
> Be praised, my Lord, through our sister Mother Earth, who feeds us and rules us, and produces various fruits with colored flowers and herbs.
>
> Be praised, my Lord, through those who forgive for love of You; through those who endure sickness and trial.
>
> Happy those who endure in peace, for by You, Most High, they will be crowned.
>
> Be praised, my Lord, through our sister Bodily Death, from whose embrace no living person can escape. Woe to those who die in mortal sin! Happy those she finds doing Your most holy will. The second death can do no harm to them.
>
> Praise and bless my Lord, and give thanks, and serve Him with great humility.

Like St. Dominic, his Spanish counterpart, St. Francis founded an order of friars (from the Latin term *frater*, meaning "brother"). Although personal devotion was key to both rules, service in the form of preaching among the laity was central among Franciscans and Dominicans alike. Indeed, Francis accepted the evangelical command to preach the gospel to the ends of the earth to the point that he made trips to Muslim lands during the time of the Crusades. But while Dominic's order proceeded increasingly on the basis of learning, the Franciscans focused on the charismatic example of their founder. What they did with that example was more revolutionary than what Francis himself did.

A Franciscan teacher named Gerardo di Borgo San Donnino published a work on the Apocalypse called *Introduction to the Eternal Gospel* (1254). As he interpreted the Revelation of John, Francis of Assisi came as the angel of the sixth seal in Revelation 6:12–17. The result was to portray the saint, not as the gentle-to-animals pantheist of some modern depictions, but as a key figure of apocalyptic fury. When the sixth seal is opened in the vision of John of Patmos, the powerful on earth are crushed:

And the kings of the earth and the magnates and the generals and the rich and the powerful and every servant and free person hid themselves in the caves and in the rocks of the mountains. And they say to the mountains and to the rocks, Fall upon us and hide us from the face of the one who sits upon the Throne and from the wrath of the Lamb. Because the great day of their wrath has come, and who is able to stand? (Revelation 6:15–16)

This was to be the dawn of the poor, identified by Gerardo di Borgo San Donnino as those Franciscans who upheld the commitment to poverty of St. Francis against the compromise of those in the order who accepted the conventions of this world.

In Gerardo's bold amalgam of vision and exegesis, the spiritual men—exemplified by Francis of Assisi—were to replace the worldly rule of the hierarchical church. Gerardo also read key passages in the Revelation in order to determine just when the rule of the poor was to begin, proceeding on the assumption, pervasive during his period, that the "days" mentioned in the Revelation are really years. In the Revelation, chapter 12, the woman, who must be the church (as Gerardo agreed with many other commentators), flees into the wilderness and is protected from the seven-headed dragon for a total of 1,260 days (Revelation 12:6). The association of images, numbers, and patterns made it obvious to Gerardo and his supporters that the millennial reign of the spiritual Franciscans would begin in the year 1260.

All other claimants to authority, including the papacy, would correspondingly be superseded, while Satan was to be consigned to the pit for a thousand years (Revelation 20:2–3). The year after the publication of Gerardo's *Introduction to the Eternal Gospel*, Pope Alexander set up a commission of cardinals to condemn the work. The movement, however, was not stopped. Successors of Gerardo announced that they would lead the *reformatio* of the church in order to restore its intended poverty and spirituality.

The prospect of any true reformation, however, depended upon a dissemination of convincing arguments and a program for change. The impetus for that came from the Renaissance, and its values were translated into religious terms by Erasmus of Rotterdam.

ERASMUS OF ROTTERDAM

Erasmus was born illegitimate, probably in 1466. His rise to a position of unrivaled influence in the world of letters and the Church marks the high-water mark of the Renaissance in reshaping the conception of the Christian faith.

Erasmus's life was shaped by the distinctive piety of the Low Countries (the Netherlands), where lay movements of asceticism flourished. Men and women joined to undertake disciplines of prayer, meditation, and good works, but without accepting monastic vows. The most prominent of these associations was the Brothers (and then Sisters) of the Common Life, founded by Gerard Groote during the fourteenth century. These communities focused on a teaching of practical mysticism called the *devotio moderna*, expressed most influentially in *The Imitation of Christ*, compiled by Thomas à Kempis after Groote's death. Women and men lived in separate communities, but each included laypeople and priests together. By Erasmus's time many houses of the movement were composed mostly of priests and accepted the Augustinian rule of monasticism. That proved to be crucial to Erasmus's development.

His father became a priest, probably after the birth of his two illegitimate sons. When Erasmus's parents died, his guardians enrolled him and his brother in a hostel for the poor run by Brothers of the Common Life. That decision virtually obliged him to join an Augustinian monastery at the age of sixteen. From the outset of his career as a monastic and a priest, an extraordinary facility in Latin was apparent, and it was put to good use by his house. He wrote a little treatise called "On contempt of the World," in which he wrote:

> I am ready to swear that there is no duty here which is not filled with happiness. There is nothing more lucrative than our poverty, nothing more free than our servitude, nothing more carefree than our labors, nothing more filled than our emptiness, nothing more broad than our narrowness, nothing more joyful than our sorrow.

From the beginning of his career to its end, his hero was Saint Jerome, who for Erasmus combined classical learning and true devotion in a single Christian philosophy of life.

That synthesis became the goal of his life, and Erasmus quickly became a passionate enthusiast for the humane letters that all humanists revered (*Against Barbarians*):

> There are those who want the Republic of Letters to be destroyed root and branch. Others are doing their best to get its power not exactly extinguished, but restricted within narrower limits. Lastly there are those who want to see the Republic preserved but utterly ruined, by themselves becoming tyrants, abrogating the laws of our fathers, and introducing foreign magistrates and behavior. The first named of these, as I see it, are those quite uncouth people who detest the whole of literature (which they call poetry) on some vague religious pretext, whether from jealousy or stupidity I cannot say. The second lot I understand to be the educated who are really uneducated, the people who somehow find other studies acceptable (that is, their own), but as for the humanities, without which all learning is blind, they hate them worse than a snake. Then there are the

last, and who else are they but the people who admire and approve of every kind of literature, especially poetry and rhetoric, but on condition that they themselves are considered the finest poets and orators—which is far from the case.

This intellectual confidence, expressed in free, elegant Latin, fitted Erasmus better to appreciative patrons and fellow authors than to monasteries. In fact, by the time he wrote his attack on behavior he no doubt had experienced at first hand, he had left the cloister to serve as Latin secretary to a prominent bishop. His extraordinary productiveness and his genius for making connections eventually won Erasmus many readers all over Europe.

English scholars first convinced Erasmus of the importance of learning Greek. He did that and went on to read Origen, one of the most challenging of patristic writers. This influence is evident in Erasmus's *Handbook of the Christian Soldier*, published in 1503:

Let us imagine, therefore, two worlds, the one only intelligible, the other visible. The intelligible, which may also be called the angelic, is the one in which God dwells with the blessed spirits, while the visible world comprises the celestial spheres and all that is contained therein. Then there is man, who contributes, as it were, a third world, participating in the other two, in the visible world through the body, and in the invisible through the soul. Since we are but pilgrims in the visible world, we should never make it our fixed abode, but should relate by a fitting comparison everything that occurs to the senses either to the angelic world or, in more practical terms, to morals and to that part of man that corresponds to the angelic. What the visible sun is here in the visible world, the divine mind is in the intelligible world and in that part of you related to it, namely, the spirit. What the moon is here is in that world the assembly of angels and blessed spirits, which they call the church triumphant, and in you it is the spirit. Whatever influence the upper world has over the earth, which lies beneath it, God exercises this same influence over your soul.

The *devotio moderna* had long insisted on the way of what it already called "our reformation," aimed at kindling "the fires of religious fervor in the cold hearts of men." Desiderius Erasmus alloyed that fervor so completely with humanistic learning in a Platonic key that he made the two virtually indistinguishable.

The *Handbook* pressed its theme without compromise. Some baptized people were "more pagan than the pagans:" "What does it matter if the body has been washed, when the soul remains defiled?" Erasmus derided those who "worship the bones of Paul preserved in a relic casket, but do not worship the mind of Paul hidden away in his writings," and the trade in "true cross" brought out invective:

> You think it an immense privilege to have a tiny particle of the cross in your home. But that is nothing compared with carrying about in your heart the mystery of the cross. If such things constitute religion, who could be more religious than the Jews? Even the most impious among them saw Jesus living in the flesh with their own eyes, heard him with their own ears, and touched him with their own hands. Who is more fortunate than Judas, who pressed his lips upon the divine mouth?

Humanists gave Erasmus an enthusiastic hearing, and as he benefited more from patronage, he grew bolder.

In Praise of Folly remains Erasmus's most famous work, a biting indictment of the posturing of the powerful in his own time. His attack on theologians, not just popular superstition, became instantly controversial, when it was published in 1511:

> In addition, they interpret hidden mysteries to suit themselves: how the world was created and designed; through what channel the stain of sin filtered down to posterity; by what means, in what measure, and how long Christ was formed in the Virgin's womb; how, in the Eucharist, accidents can subsist without a domicile. But this sort of question has been discussed threadbare. There are others more worthy of great and enlightened theologians (as they call themselves) which really can rouse them to action if they come their way. What was the exact moment of divine generation? Are there several filiations in Christ? Is it a possible proposition that God the Father could hate his Son? Could God have taken on the form of a woman, a devil, a donkey, a gourd, or a flint stone? If so, how could a gourd have preached sermons, performed miracles, and been nailed to the cross? And what would Peter have consecrated if he had consecrated when the body of Christ still hung on the cross?

Erasmus not only targeted abuses of piety, but the scholastic method of those who attempted to parse Christian doctrine with the philosophy and method of Aristotle. For him, that represented a confusion of the intelligible world with the visible world.

Against the scholastics, Erasmus proposed the *philosophia Christi* or *doctrina Evangelica*—the transformative power of truth shining into emotions as well as minds. His dedication to this principle came to fruition in his *Novum Instrumentum*, his edition of the New Testament in Greek with his own Latin translation and explanatory notes. He referred to the text as an *instrumentum*, as Tertullian had during the second century, because for him the New Testament was an "instrument" of change, not just words to be studied. And change through the ages, in crucial questions such as the theology of the Eucharist, the discipline of divorce, the marriage of clergy, and the power of popes, was a simple fact of history and experience.

Erasmus conceived a particular hatred for Pope Julius II (1503–13), a pontiff who went to war against fellow Christians to extend papal lands and sold church offices as well as indulgences in order to finance his patronage of the arts. But while Erasmus went to the extent of penning *Julius Excluded from Heaven*, events were to prove that the conduct of popes was not merely a matter of their individual characters. Julius's excesses, as Erasmus judged them, included engaging Michelangelo to decorate the Sistine Chapel, adjacent to a new papal residence. That was part of a program of building that extended over several papacies, a projection of faith's character in stone and paint that embodied the values of the Renaissance.

The restoration and extension of St. Peter's Basilica in Rome had been more or less constantly undertaken since its construction in the fourth century. But Julius II and his architect Donato Bramante effectively wanted to see a cathedral worthy of the Renaissance. The new St. Peter's was only dedicated in 1626, more than a century after Julius's death. Even Michelangelo's legendary powers (he took over as chief of works between 1546 until his death in 1564) did not see it through to anything like completion.

The achievement was as expensive as it was heroic, and during much of the earlier period of construction, the papacy had a greater ambition for patronage than it could meet from its own resources.

Julius II's successor, Giovanni de' Medici of Florence, took the name of Leo X. He unsuccessfully called for a new crusade, but proved a highly effective patron of St. Peter's. In order to finance his huge campaign, Leo authorized the increased sale of indulgences; that marketing device was to prove the pivot on which the Renaissance became the Reformation.

INDULGENCES

The theology of the indulgence turned on exactly the kind of Aristotelian logic that Erasmus and other Christian humanists despised. The whole enterprise was predicated on the scholastic method. Blanket indulgences had been introduced at the time of the Crusades, as a promise that the crusaders' sacrifice would bring them remission of their sins. But as time went on, popes claimed that activities well short of martyrdom—such as making pilgrimages and giving money—could release a departed soul from some of its punishment in purgatory. The idea was that, although hell was outside the pope's jurisdiction, one's sentence to purgatory—a temporal punishment, for a set period of time after death in view of sins committed during life—could be shortened by papal authority. Pope Clement VI, forced by French power and turmoil in Italy to reside at Avignon rather than Rome, articulated this theology in the bull *Unigenitus* in 1343. Sales of indulgences made the construction of the papal palace in Avignon possible and formed a key aspect of the growing financial network of the papacy.

Leo X readily embraced this method for the extension of St. Peter's on a scale worthy of the Medicis. He promulgated an indulgence for this purpose and at the same time entered into a lucrative arrangement with Archbishop Albert of Mainz. Albert, at twenty-seven, was already Archbishop of Magdeburg and he needed Rome's permission (called a dispensation) to combine ecclesiastical offices. He paid for this dispensation by taking a loan from the Fugger banking house in Augsburg and brought in Johann Tetzel, a

Dominican friar, to sell indulgences, splitting the revenue to pay for Leo's building project and his own loan.

By 1517 Tetzel had a well-established and well-deserved reputation for the sale of indulgences. His big claim to fame was the assertion that, armed with his indulgences, one could help—not only one-self—but also departed relatives out of purgatory. He paraded into town with bells literally ringing, banners of the papal arms, huge red crosses, preaching, it was claimed, "Once you hear the money ring, the soul from purgatory is free to spring."

Wittenberg, a market and university town, was a likely target of opportunity, but Tetzel was prohibited from going there. Frederick called "the Wise," the Elector of Saxony, had his own fine collection of relics—bits of bone and other holy remains—that assured him revenues that he had no wish to see diluted. For the little fee required to reverence a relic, Frederick's subjects could enjoy indulgences on a local scale. Contemplating his collection of 5,005 items could bring 1,443 years of exemption from purgatory. Tetzel and Frederick were in a conflict of interests, although each saw the value of indulgences.

But an Augustinian priest in Frederick's territory had been stirring up controversy over the question of whether indulgences were really permissible at all. In retrospect, the passion of the two sides may seem difficult to understand, especially in the light of all the debates that the Christian humanists had long pursued. But his personal character and his position in German society made Martin Luther into the indispensable agent of the Reformation.

The son of a copper-miner whose family managed to support him through studies in the liberal arts and law at Erfurt University, Luther broke with his father's wishes by entering an Augustinian monastery and living as a recluse. As much as Erasmus read St. Augustine for his Platonism, Luther read him for guidance on the experience of conversion. He developed a passion for the study of the Scriptures, learning Hebrew and Greek in the course of his study and teaching, which focused especially on the Psalms and Paul's Letter to the Romans. The key to Paul's theology and to human experience, he believed, was "The just shall live by faith" (Romans 1:17, citing Habakkuk 2:4). Direct trust in God, apart from reliance on the conventions of earthly authorities, was the only path of justice, the single means to salvation.

MARTIN LUTHER

Luther lectured on Romans in 1515, and by the time of Tetzel's campaign, he had found a big local audience. He wrote to a friend in May 1517:

> My theology—which is St. Augustine's—is getting on and is dominant in the university. God has done it. Aristotle is going downhill and perhaps he will go all the way down to hell. It amazes me that so few people want lectures on the *Sentences* of Peter Lombard. Nobody will go to hear a lecture unless the lecturer is teaching my theology—which is the theology of the Bible, of St. Augustine, and of all true theologians of the Church. I am quite sure that the Church will never be reformed unless we get rid of canon law, scholastic theology, philosophy and logic as they are studied today, and put something else in their place.

Although he was simply a parish priest and a professor at a provincial university, in his mid-thirties Martin Luther was thinking on the grandest of scales.

Johann Tetzel's activities came to Luther's attention through the people of his local church. He reacted to what he told them as their priest and took up the academic cudgels as a proud professor. He wrote first, in suitably deferential terms, to Archbishop Albert and in the absence of a response proposed certain theses for discussion and debate. Eventually they were posted on the door of the church in Wittenberg on the Feast of All Saints in 1517. He named his proposal, "Disputation on the Power and Efficacy of Indulgences," which ran to ninety-five theses, the popular name of his notice.

THE "NINETY-FIVE THESES"

The first ten propositions set the tone for the whole and demonstrate the depth of Luther's challenge to the whole system of papal indulgence:

1. When our Lord and Master, Jesus Christ, said "Repent," He called for the entire life of believers to be one of penitence.

2. The word cannot properly be understood as referring to the sacrament of penance, i.e., confession and satisfaction, as administered by the clergy.

3. Yet its meaning is not restricted to penitence in one's heart; for such penitence is null unless it produces outward signs in various mortifications of the flesh.

4. As long as hatred of self abides (i.e., true inward penitence) the penalty of sin abides, viz., until we enter the kingdom of heaven.

5. The pope has neither the will nor the power to remit any penalty beyond those imposed either at this own discretion or by canon law.

6. The pope himself cannot remit guilt, but only declare and confirm that it has been remitted by God; or, at most, he can remit it in cases reserved to his discretion. Except for these cases, the guilt remains untouched.

7. God never remits guilt to anyone without, at the same time, making him humbly submissive to the priest, His representative.

8. The penitential canons apply only to men who are still alive, and, according to the canons themselves, none applies to the dead.

9. Accordingly, the Holy Spirit, acting in the person of the pope, manifests grace to us, by the fact that the papal regulations always cease to apply at death, or in any hard case.

10. It is a wrongful act, due to ignorance, when priests retain the canonical penalties on the dead in purgatory.

Luther deployed all his considerable forensic skill to probe into discovering how God can forgive and—equally mysterious—how human beings can move beyond their self-loathing without usurping the power of God.

The vehemence of Luther's theses reflects his passionate commitment to the principle of "justification by faith alone." In his experience, complete and personal trust in God cut through doubt in oneself and inner torment. Even Luther, however, was unprepared for the level of controversy that erupted over his theses. He famously complained, "The song was pitched in too high a key for my voice." His character was only one dimension of the controversy; the other was where the dispute had broken out. Frederick of Saxony was not a supporter of Luther's theology on indulgences, but he was a proud local ruler suspicious of incursions into his territory. He supported the "impertinent monk," as Archbishop Albert called Luther, who had annoyed his ecclesiastical superiors.

Pope Leo sent Cardinal Cajetan as his legate to deal with the case. Since he was a Dominican, as Tetzel was, there was no doubt about the side Cajetan would come down on. But because the theology of indulgences (especially as preached by Tetzel) was questionable, Cajetan pitched the dispute in terms of papal authority. Inadvertently, he colluded with Luther in framing the debate as the limits of the Pope's power in relation to God.

The exchange transpired in a volatile atmosphere. Luther's theses had been translated into German, and he enjoyed enormous popular support. Over the years, his direct, passionate prose became a benchmark of Reformation preaching and the pride of German nationalism. Tetzel, although honored by Rome, was afraid to appear in public. Luther's intransigence, however, invited countermeasures.

The fear of heresy went hand in hand with the fear of revolt. Jan Huss had been burned at the stake in 1415 for his combined program of Bible translation and local revolution, and Czech nationalism remained a problem a century later. The Inquisition, the burning of witches, pogroms against Jews, and the expulsion of Jews from Spain in 1492 all represent Catholic Europe's violent fear of apostasy and insurrection. Luther's public posed a greater threat to the pope than Luther himself.

Leo attempted to resolve the issue by diplomacy, while Luther called for a General Council of the Church, whose authority he said exceeded the pope's. Meanwhile, writing *To the Christian Nobility of the German Nation* in 1520, he called on kings and princes to resist papal incursions, including indulgences. All Christians are priests according to the teaching of the New Testament, so it was right for rulers to use their civic power to uphold the authority of the Bible.

On June 15, 1520 Leo issued *Exsurge Domine*, excommunicating Luther unless he recanted and ordering his books burned. That bull was as inevitable as Luther's reaction: He responded with a tract on

Christian liberty that was designed to defend his position and burned the pope's edict in public, along with copies of canon law and other papal decrees. That act and the raucous popular violence he attracted required some action by Charles V, the young and newly chosen Holy Roman Emperor (and therefore the titular ruler of Germany). Luther had appealed to him in his call *To the Christian Nobility of the German Nation*, but the emperor was also the king of Spain, newly emerged as a dominant Catholic power, and he could only see the events swirling around Luther as threats to the unity and stability of his domains as a whole. He convened a Diet (that is, an assembly) at Worms in 1521.

Luther attended under an imperial safe conduct. The emperor asked him to recant on April 18. Luther replied:

> Unless I am proved wrong by Scriptures or by evident reason, then I am a prisoner in conscience to the Word of God. I cannot retract and I will not retract. To go against the conscience is neither safe nor right. God help me. Amen.

Later that same year, despite suffering depression and having to live concealed in Wartberg, Luther began his translation of the Bible into German, a pillar of the Reformation, as important to its intellectual life as his hymns were to its liturgical life.

Reformation meant revolution in several ways. The liturgy itself was reformed, beginning with the practice of permitting laypeople to receive both bread and wine during Eucharist, rather than reserving the wine for priests alone. Priestly vestments were simplified, priests were permitted to marry, and zealots for change began to demolish altars they considered too ornate. On a more systematic level, civic authorities confiscated ecclesiastical funds and began to administer them for social services. When Luther returned to Wittenberg, it was as much to contain the Reformation as to spread it.

THE PEASANTS' REVOLTS

When a series of peasant revolts broke out in the south of Germany in 1524–25, Luther responded with his characteristic passion in *Against the Rioting Peasants*:

> These times are so extraordinary that a prince can more easily win heaven by bloodshed than by prayer.

To his mind, the priesthood of all believers, which made Christians of every station individually accountable before God and jointly responsible for the Church, needed to be exercised within the natural authorities of this world. He accepted the justice of many of the grievances cited by the rebellious peasants, but condemned their attempt to seize authority. His modulated argument, which urged restraint on princes and called for the use of the sword as a last resort, was distorted by publishers who gave his pamphlet the title, *Against the Murdering, Thieving Hordes of Peasants*.

In this realm of theological politics, Luther—himself no politician—set out a position that also became emblematic of the Reformation as a whole. He had already written of *Secular Authority* in 1523:

> All who are not Christian belong to the kingdom of the world and are under the law. Since few believe and still fewer live a Christian life, do not resist the evil, and themselves do no evil, God has provided for non-Christians a different government outside the Christian estate and God's kingdom, and has subjected them to the sword, so that, even though they would do so, they cannot practice their wickedness, and that, if they do, they may not do it without fear or in peace and prosperity. Even so a wild, savage beast is fastened with chains and bands, so that it cannot bite and tear as is its wont, although it gladly would do so; whereas a tame and gentle beast does not require this, but without chains and bands is nevertheless harmless. If it were not so, seeing that the whole world is evil and that among thousands there is scarcely one true Christian, men would devour one another, and no one would preserve wife and child, support himself, and serve God; and thus the world would be reduced to chaos. For this reason, God has ordained the two governments; the spiritual, which by the Holy Spirit under Christ makes Christians and pious people, and the secular, which restrains the unchristian and wicked so that they must needs keep the peace outwardly, even against their will.

A wily monarch could easily press such a teaching to his own advantage. That was exactly the case with Christian II of Denmark, who invited Lutheran preachers from Wittenberg to Denmark. His attempt to extend his power over Sweden led to revolt there under Gustavus Vasa, and Sweden established a national church along the lines of the Reformation in 1531, guided by Olaus Petri, who had personally studied with Luther. The settlements in Norway and Finland were comparable in religious terms.

The Reformation fomented a brisk nationalism that could decay into civil war, the division of traditional hegemonies, and uprisings of popular heretics, while it also offered rulers such as Gustavus and Christian undoubted opportunities. Charles V, as we have already seen, sided with the papacy, despite Luther's hopes. François I of France permitted bishops such as Guillaume Briçonnet of Meaux to pursue some of the aims of the Reformation, within the polity of the Catholic Church. In England, the papacy found a staunch defender in Henry VIII, who—prompted by Thomas More, Erasmus's friend—in 1521 wrote *The Defense of the Seven Sacraments against Martin Luther*, dedicating the work to Leo X. The grateful pontiff bestowed the title "Defender of the Faith" on Henry, which is borne by British monarchs to this day. In contrast to these national sovereigns, all committed to varying degrees to papal authority, the German princes joined in a "Protest" against the emperor and his allies at the Diet of Speyer in 1529, and they linked up in 1531 into an alliance called the Schmalkadic League.

With the exception of Scandinavia, the prospects of the Protestants in Europe looked precarious. Both in Rome and in England, however, events took a surprising course, which put Henry and the pope who eventually succeeded Leo X in 1523, Clement VII, at loggerheads. Henry's wife had delivered only one child that survived, a girl. Five children had been stillborn. Henry desperately wanted a male heir to inherit his throne in order to avoid wars of succession. He claimed that his plight was divine punishment for his having married his brother's widow, against the teaching of the Bible (Leviticus 18:16; 20:21). It was within the pope's power, as defended by Henry, to declare the marriage invalid, and there were many precedents for such declarations for reasons of state.

But after 1527, there were excellent reasons of state for Clement to deny the request. In that year, the troops of Charles V had sacked Rome, as part of his extension of imperial power, capturing the pope at the same time. Catherine of Aragon, Henry's wife, was also Charles's aunt. By the summer of 1529 the papal legates commissioned by Clement still had reached no decision in regard to the marriage and Cardinal Compeggio adjourned the case, on the improbable grounds that the British summer was too hot.

Henry acted in that same year to pressure Clement to act on his behalf, chipping away at papal power through acts of Parliament. This required no great statesmanship; Parliament was always ready to go much further in the direction of Reformation teaching than Henry was. By 1531, Parliament insisted that clergy could not administer canon law independently of the crown. "As far as the law of Christ allows," they declared, the king was "especial Protector," "even supreme Head of the Church." In 1533, appeals from England to Rome were prohibited, and in the same year, Thomas Cranmer—as archbishop of Canterbury—annulled Henry's marriage to Catherine, and the king married Anne Boleyn.

Events in England corresponded to new outbreaks of much less orderly demands for change on mainland Europe. In Münster (Westphalia), Bernard Rothman, an Anabaptist leader, took control of the city council in 1533 and followed the teaching of an Anabaptist recently arrived in Münster named Jan Mattys and a self-styled prophet named John of Leyden. Anabaptists insisted that, according to the New Testament, baptism is a spiritual rebirth that only believers committed to Christ can enjoy. John went beyond that program, however, declaring himself King and sanctioning polygamy along the lines of the patriarchs of Israel. His revolution encouraged outbreaks in other cities until the local bishop's army killed him in 1535.

François I of France had by this time already executed people on the charge of heresy, but after 18 October 1534, his policy became more vigorous. That morning, placards were found in Paris, Orléans, and Blois denouncing him and his régime as well as Catholic practices. Blaming Protestant elements in his country, François had dozens of suspects burned after he made a procession to the cathedral of Notre Dame in Paris, and Protestant leaders made an exodus from France, especially to Switzerland.

The Swiss Reformation by this time displayed a more coordinated aspect than Luther's movement. Ulrich Zwingli of Zurich embraced Luther's writings from 1519, but he adhered to a program of Reform that was more biblical and more militant than Luther's. (In fact, the "Reformed" churches defined themselves in distinction to Lutheran churches as well as Roman churches.) In his view, Christians were not only to correct their practices with reference to the Scriptures; the Scriptures ought to sanction their practices. He opposed Luther's teaching on the Lord's Supper or Eucharist, for example, because he refused to believe in any substantial change in bread and wine or in Jesus being present in them. The body and blood of Christ were apprehended spiritually, more in the manner of the Christian humanism of Erasmus. Zwingli and Luther never reconciled after a public dispute in 1529.

Supported by the civic council in Zurich, Zwingli engaged in a program of reforming the city itself, in a manner that came to typify Reformed churches. The militancy of Zwingli was such that he took to the field in helmet and sword against his Catholic opponents. He was captured in 1531, and drawn and quartered; his ashes were scattered after his corpse was burned.

But the Reform prospered in Strasbourg under Martin Bucer, and was introduced to Geneva by Guillaume Farel, who had left France and arrived in Geneva under the protection of the Berne city council. By 1535, Geneva was an independent city, no longer obliged to adhere to the authority of the local bishop. The following year Farel invited a fellow French reformer, Jean Calvin, to remain in Geneva.

CALVINISM

Jean Calvin had to struggle to work out his theological and organizational principles at the same time as he implemented them in a contentious political environment. But his two major works, *The Institutes of the Christian Religion* and the *Ecclesiastical Ordinances*, which he urged the town council to pass, are an enduring contribution to Christian faith and polity. The first of these works was published in 1536, and the *Ordinances* took recognizable shape in 1541, but they were life works that Calvin devoted himself to until his death in 1564.

Calvin conceived a scheme in which pastors appointed teachers in consultation with the city government. The civic council, in turn, appointed elders in consultation with the pastors. The purpose of the elders was to survey the morals of the city—public and private—and act against such dangers as heresy and popery as well as dancing and prostitution. The Scottish advocate of the Reform, John Knox, called Geneva "the most perfect school of Christ that ever was on earth since the days of the Apostles."

Calvin's genius was theological as well as organizational. He stated the principle of justification by faith lucidly:

> To declare that by him alone we are accounted righteous, what else is this but to lodge our righteousness in Christ's obedience, because the obedience of Christ is reckoned to us as if it were our own? For this reason, it seems to me that Ambrose beautifully stated an example of this righteousness in the blessing of Jacob: Noting that, as he did not of himself deserve the right of the firstborn, concealed in his brother's clothing and wearing his brother's coat, which gave out an agreeable odor (Genesis 27:27), he ingratiated himself with his father, so that to his own benefit he received the benefit while impersonating another. And we in like manner hide under the precious purity of our firstborn brother, Christ, so that we may be attested righteous in God's sight. Here are the words of Ambrose: "That Isaac smelled the odor of the garments perhaps means that we are justified not by works but by faith, since the weakness of the flesh is a hindrance to works, but the brightness of faith, which merits the pardon of sons, overshadows the error of deeds." And this is indeed the truth, for in order that we may appear before God's face unto salvation we must smell sweetly with his odor, and our vices must be covered and buried by his perfection.

The logic, elegance, and feeling of this explanation help account for Calvin's deep influence on the people of Geneva and for the seamless combination of emotion and thought in the best of Reformed theology.

But Calvin knew, and knew all too well from practical experience, that people can wear faith as a mask, concealing the truth about themselves even from themselves. An even more careful reader of Augustine than he was of Ambrose, he investigated the consequences of this hard truth:

> Yet what Augustine writes is nonetheless true: that all who are estranged from the religion of the one God, however admirable they may be regarded on account of their reputation for virtue, not only deserve no reward but rather punishment, because by the pollution of their hearts they defile God's good works. For even though they are God's instruments for the preservation of human society in righteousness, continence, friendship, temperance, fortitude, and prudence, yet they carry out the good works of God very badly. For they are restrained from evildoing not by genuine zeal for good but either by mere ambition or by self-love, or some other perverse motive. Therefore, since by the very impurity of men's hearts these good works have been corrupted as from their source, they ought no more to be reckoned among the virtues than the vices that commonly deceive on account of their affinity and likeness to virtue. In short, when we remember the constant end of that which is right—namely, to serve God—whatever strives to another end already deservedly loses the name "right." Therefore, because they do not look to the goal that God's wisdom prescribes, what they do, though it seems good in the doing, yet by its perverse intention is sin.

This rigorous focus on the goal of life gives Calvin's thought its characteristically teleological character, because God alone could truly know the end of any human being.

God knew the outcome of all choices any human being might make. On that Augustine and Calvin were agreed. Predestination, to salvation or damnation, was a matter of God being God: "It is a question of the secret judgments of God whose brightness not only dazzles the minds of men when they presume to approach them too closely, but destroys and consumes them utterly."

By this time, Protestantism and Roman Catholicism, both products of the Catholic Church of the Middle Ages, had emerged with different structures of belief. Obviously, they shared many beliefs in detail, but their definition of the central tenet that gave faith coherence differed. Justification by faith alone and papal supremacy in the order of the Church had become mutually exclusive principles.

The accession of Edward VI in 1547 opened the floodgates of reform in England. Henry VIII's Six Articles were repealed, and Protestant ministers were free to remove images from their churches, give wine at Communion as well as bread, and live openly with their wives. Cranmer was responsible primarily for the *Book of Common Prayer* in 1549 and again in 1552. One difference between the two books is instructive. While the 1549 Communion has the minister say, "The Body of our Lord Jesus Christ which was given for thee, preserve thy body and soul unto everlasting life," from 1552 he was to say, "Take and eat this in remembrance that Christ died for thee, and feed on him in thy heart by faith, with thanksgiving." The growing influence of Reformed rather than Lutheran teaching is evident. In Scotland, John Knox even managed to force Cranmer to agree in writing that kneeling to receive the sacrament did not imply "any real and essential presence there being of Christ's natural body and blood." The trenchantly Reformed character of the Anglican Church was now undeniable, although far less complete than in Calvin's Geneva.

From 1542, papal policy also took a trenchant form. Pope Paul III's bull *Licet ab initio* established an Inquisition in Italy (on the Spanish model) in order to root out heresy. The Inquisition authorized the by now traditional methods of confiscating property, imprisonment, torture, and execution. Cardinal Carafa, who had initiated the plan, guided the Inquisition in its attack on Protestants, Anabaptists, and those whose orthodoxy was suspect. His decrees were explicit: "No man is to lower himself by showing toleration toward any sort of heretic, least of all a Calvinist." Carafa became Pope Paul IV in 1555; he began the *Index of Prohibited Books*—including all of Erasmus and the *Decameron* of Boccaccio—that resulted in the burning of tens of thousands of volumes, and instituted the rule that Jews were to live in ghettos and wear yellow hats. Paul IV's conduct was extreme, and public demonstrations greeted his death in 1559. But even toward the end of Paul III's reign as pope, the consolidation of papal power in the realm of doctrine became the chief characteristic of Roman Catholic theology.

From 1545, successive popes convened councils of the Church at Trent (south of the Alps) in a series of three sessions until 1563. From the outset, the bishops who attended (only 28 at first, but more than 200 by the close of proceedings) denied Protestant doctrine and went on to canonize the Latin Vulgate and the Latin Mass together with Transubstantiation. In reaction to Calvin's *Institutes,* they made Thomas Aquinas the premier theologian of systematic doctrine. But at the same time, these meetings also achieved genuine reform and represent what is called the Catholic Reformation or the Counter-Reformation. The bishops addressed the problem of absentee clergy and immorality in the Church hierarchy, provided for a new emphasis on preaching and on education at all levels, and abolished the office for the sale of indulgences that Johann Tetzel had occupied.

The Jesuits, as members of the Society of Jesus came to be called, played a key role in these developments. In 1521, a Spanish soldier named Ignatius Loyola was wounded in the French siege of Pamplona. His smashed leg meant the end of his military career, but he determined to continue as a soldier of Christ, writing in his *Spiritual Exercises* of how a person might take Jesus' sufferings on himself, in order to heal his soul and submit it in obedience to the Church as the Bride of Christ. In 1540, Paul III authorized the Society of Jesus, and it proved an ideal instrument of the Catholic Reformation.

Loyola appealed to "all those who want to fight under the banner of God in our Society, which we wish to designate with the name of Jesus, and who are willing to serve solely God and his vicar on earth." In his *Spiritual Exercises*, he adopted the *devotio moderna* (and in particularly the *Imitation of Christ* of Thomas à Kempis) to a new aim: complete obedience to the pope as the divinely appointed "vicar on earth."

After 1542, religion divided Europe between Roman Catholic and Protestant Christianity; sometimes the fault line ran between nation-states, and sometimes within them. In every case, however, the emerging theologies called on the force, if necessary the violent force, of secular power in order to protect the truth of their positions. In the Protestant view, the very purpose of any state was, as Luther said, to "set free the Christian corrective measures to punish sin, and bring the devil's deceits and wiles to the light of day" (*To the Christian*

Nobility of the German Nation). In the Roman Catholic view of Ignatius
Loyola, only obedience to the pope, God's "vicar on earth," could
transcend the violent factionalism and warfare of suffering Europe.

The issue of faith had made its way into the center of controversy regarding religion, the principal issue during the period.
But the difference between Roman Catholics and Protestants over
the issue of faith had less to do with how to define it, than with
how it fitted in the system of Christianity. For Roman Catholics,
faith emerged as the central ethical requirement of religion, with the
elements of faith articulated by the sacraments and the hierarchy:

Protestants, on the other hand, saw faith as the conditioning factor
that authorized the existence of any sacramental or hierarchal authority.
The ethical application of the system was not faith, but salvation,
which each believer was to work out in conduct. Once a believer had
been justified by faith, the single ritual power that truly remained
for Protestantism, ethics emerged as a product of being saved:

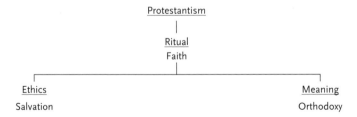

Precisely because both Catholics and Protestant laid claim to the
heritage of Orthodoxy, and each found a place for the centrality of
faith, although each in a different place, their confrontation was

inevitable. Given the ethos of Holy War that had already been established, violence was the predictable result.

CONSCIENCE

By the time the Council of Trent ceased meeting in 1563, the nation-states of Europe had chosen sides over the issue of religion or were in the process of doing so. Religious dedication translated into armed violence; the Enlightenment emerged as a movement dedicated to the rule of Reason (regularly capitalized during this whole period) in a time when Europe might have drowned in pessimism.

Spain and France were as committed to Roman Catholicism as England and Scandinavia were to the Protestant cause. Italy's city-states continued to vie with the Vatican (as the papal court was called) for prominence, but their devotion to their traditional faith was secure. Germany was deeply divided among Catholic and Protestant counties; present-day Belgium was split down the middle.

Each side of the divide, Protestant and Catholic, was convinced that its version of Christianity alone was valid and that no government could legitimately rule without the endorsement of God. As a result, nation-states, city-states, counties, and regions purged their own populations so as to become as purely Catholic or Protestant as they could. They also fought one another, advancing their religious and political agendas with implacable and often murderous force.

In France both Protestants and Catholics—each represented in the aristocracy and even the royal line—armed themselves for war against one another. In 1563 the assassination of the Catholic Francis, duc de Guise brought on a civil war with many atrocities. The most famous of them was the Saint Bartholomew's Day Massacre, when Protestant leaders were invited to Paris in 1572 to celebrate a marriage between the daughter of Catherine de' Medici, of the Catholic royal house, and Henry of Navarre, a Protestant. Their massacre at what should have been a reconciling marriage only inflamed the war, which was finally stopped when the same Henry prevailed on the field of battle. He announced his conversion to Roman Catholicism in order to reign as Henry IV from 1594. Four years later, he issued the Edict of Nantes, which offered toleration to Protestant practice.

Spanish power reached its height under the Catholic Philip II (1556–98). He became king of Portugal as well as of Spain in 1581, commanded an empire in the New World, and ruled territories in the Netherlands and in Italy. The range of Spanish power proved fateful in the unfolding pattern of war in Europe. In 1571, Philip's navy proved the decisive force in the battle with the Ottoman fleet. Married to Mary I of England (1553–58), he aspired to put down the Reformation there with her active cooperation. When Mary died, Philip proposed marriage to Elizabeth I (1558–1603) but the daughter of Ann Boleyn predictably rejected him. His response was to prepare an invasion of England. In 1588 his Armada foundered in the unpredictable English Channel amidst the smaller English merchant vessels converted for battle.

The Armada had been on the way to the Netherlands, part of Philip's realm and—he hoped—a bridgehead for assaulting England. But the increasingly Protestant Netherlands themselves revolted and achieved independence from Spain by the beginning of the seventeenth century. In addition, Sweden establish virtual control of the Baltic during this period, and its king, Gustavus Adolphus (1611–32), was one of the preeminent Protestant leaders of Europe, in alliance with both England and the Netherlands. Power at sea therefore became a Protestant trademark.

Sweden's attractiveness to the English and Dutch also lay in its counterweight to Denmark, although Denmark was itself a Protestant nation. As Europe geared up for war, it became plain that religion alone would not determine who was an ally, who an enemy, and when battle would be engaged. Although the battles, atrocities, and intellectual combat of this period are commonly called "The Wars of Religion," this period saw secular concerns masquerading under the cover of religion in ways that had not been the case earlier. In addition to the extreme violence of these wars, they marked the emergence of considerations of state predominating over matters of faith.

THE THIRTY YEARS' WAR, AND THE MONOPOLY OF VIOLENCE IN NATION-STATES

The election of Ferdinand Habsburg as king of Bohemia pre-cipitated Protestant rebellion, when Ferdinand did not deliver the toleration he promised. In 1618, two of his advisers were thrown out the window of the royal palace in Prague, and for thirty years violence spiraled out of anyone's control.

At first Ferdinand seemed invincible; he had Prague sacked in 1620. His victory emboldened Spain under Philip III to seize its territory in the Netherlands. The intervention of the Danish king Christian IV on behalf of the Protestants only resulted in Christian's defeat in 1629. The following year, however, Gustavus Adolphus of Sweden entered the fray, supported with aid from Catholic France (designed to resist the power of Spain, despite its being a Catholic nation). In a brilliant campaign—that also carried out sacking in revenge for sacking—Gustavus conquered most of central and northern Germany by the time of his own death in battle in 1632.

Gustavus's victories signaled the erosion of Habsburg power. Even France actually declared war on Catholic Spain in 1635, and fighting seesawed in the Netherlands. Meanwhile, the Dutch fleet destroyed much of Spain's navy and Portugal seceded from its union with Spain in 1640. The Spanish empire disintegrated in the attempt to extend its power beyond its capacity to control events, territories, or the loyalties of those it sought to conquer—a lesson in the fragility of empire.

By 1648 an exhausted Europe settled its war in the Peace of Westphalia, which was signed at Münster. The Netherlands gained statehood and Switzerland achieved independence. Both France and Sweden acquired territory. Most importantly, however, each nation gained autonomous sovereignty, the power of each nation-state to reach a religious settlement, based on Catholicism, Protestantism, or the toleration of the two. That was a real gain from a war that cost millions of lives, Europe's last great war of religion. The Thirty Years' War therefore gave Europe what has been called the royal state, an unprecedented concentration of power in the hands of the sovereign ruler, conceived to reign by the divine right of kings.

THE DIVINE RIGHT OF KINGS

James VI of Scotland, who later became James I of England, wrote a tract in 1598 called "The True Law of Free Monarchies," in which he set out a theology of divine right:

As there is not a thing so necessary to be known by the people of any land, next the knowledge of their God, as the right knowledge of their allegiance, according to the form of government established among them, especially in a Monarchy (which form of government, as resembling the Divinity, approaches nearest to perfection, as all the learned and wise men from the beginning have agreed upon; Unity being the perfection of all things). So has ignorance, and (which is worse) the seduced opinion of the multitude blinded by them who think themselves able to teach and instruct the ignorant, procured the rack and overthrow of sundry flourishing Commonwealths; and heaped heavy calamities, threatening utter destruction upon others. And the smiling success, that unlawful rebellions have oftentimes had against Princes in ages past (such has been the misery, and iniquity of the time) has by way of practice strengthened many in their error ... as hereafter shall be proved at more length. And among others, no Commonwealth, that ever has been since the beginning, has had greater need of the true knowledge of this ground, than this our so long disordered, and distracted Commonwealth has: the misknowledge hereof being the only spring, from whence have flowed so many endless calamities, miseries, and confusions, as is better felt by many, than the cause thereof well known, and deeply considered. The natural zeal therefore that I bear to this my native country, with the great pity I have to see the so-long disturbance there for lack of the true knowledge of this ground (as I have said before) has compelled me at last to break silence, to discharge my conscience to you my dear countrymen herein, that knowing the ground from whence these your many endless troubles have proceeded, as well as you have already too-long tasted the bitter fruits thereof, you may by knowledge, and eschewing of the cause escape, and divert the lamentable effects that ever necessarily follow thereupon. I have chosen then only to set down in this short Treatise, the true ground of the mutual duty, and allegiance between a free and absolute Monarch and his people; not to trouble your patience with answering the contrary propositions, which some have not been ashamed to set down in writ, to the poisoning of the infinite number of simple souls, and their own perpetual, and well deserved infamie ...

In James's mind, ruling was what kings were for, not answering arguments that contradicted his assertion of sovereign power. Freedom in his mind and in the absolutist ideology involved the unconstrained exertion of power by the monarch, not any rights attributed to his subjects.

James's belief that kings were free of constraint from their subjects was not at all unique. In 1614, the Estates General in France agreed that the king is sovereign in France and holds his crown from God only. Bureaucracy, tax, and military expenditure all grew at a rapid pace as a result of the acceptance of royal and national absolutism, upsetting the old decentralized web of obligations that Europe had evolved during the Middle Ages. Europe's religions also took on distinctively national characteristics during this period, as sovereigns were believed to embody the faith as well as the power of their people.

Europe's political and religious character changed under the force of arms. In France, popular frustrations led to the uprising called the "*Fronde*" (a name for a slingshot) in the same year as the Peace of Westphalia was signed. The *Fronde* successfully occupied Paris, but deteriorating conditions there made it easy for Louis XIV, only thirteen years old and hastily declared to be mature enough to rule, to order the capture of the city. His welcome there was an indication that monarchy was the agreed paradigm of rule, even among those who rebelled against particular rulers.

By the time of the *Fronde*, England had already been submerged in a civil war for six years. Charles I and a Parliament dominated by Puritans (as partisans of Reformed Christianity were called) could not settle their argument over whether Reformation principles should govern the church strictly. The Puritan program of replacing the hierarchy of bishops and archbishops with elected presbyters was never fully implemented, but the Westminster Confession of 1646 articulated Parliament's Calvinist aspirations. Under General Oliver Cromwell's coup, Charles was executed in 1649, and England became a commonwealth of citizens instead of a monarchy of subjects.

To a growing extent, theologians in the West began to show that the thought of Orthodoxy in the East had begun to influence them. That influence is best articulated in the pages of a cumulative book of monastic wisdom called the *Philokalia*, a term that means "love of beauty." Owing its foundation to the spiritual advice of Origen during the third century, this anthology of contemplation was continually developed until its publication in the West in 1782. With the growing influence and power of Russia under the Romanov dynasty, Orthodox conceptions became better known in the West.

THE *PHILOKALIA*

St. Theodoros the Great Ascetic, who lived during the ninth century and became bishop of Edessa, is one of the most influential teachers represented in the *Philokalia*. A staunch opponent of collective monasticism, which he considered a distraction from true contemplation, Theodoros centered his thought on the capacity of human beings to become godlike, since by their nature they reflected the divine. As Basil the Great (c. 330–79 CE) said, "I am a creature that has received the command to become a god." This process is known as *theosis*, or becoming divine. The analogy of human conscience to the divine became a characteristic conception in the West from the time of John Milton.

One of Cromwell's most effective propagandists was John Milton, who published "The Tenure of Kings and Magistrates" two weeks after the execution of Charles I, arguing that society was constituted by a covenant between ruler and ruled which was greater than any party. Despite the brevity of Cromwell's experiment, the conception that Milton developed proved over the long term an effective counterweight to the divine right of kings.

THE PURITAN COVENANT AND INDIVIDUAL LIBERTY

The displacement of divine right by a covenantal principle of governance became emblematic of the Enlightenment and Milton stated it with elegant aggression:

No man who knows aught, can be so stupid to deny that all men were naturally born free, being the image and resemblance of God himself, and were by privilege above all the creatures, born to command and not to obey: and that they lived so. Till from the root of Adam's transgression, falling among themselves to do wrong and violence, and foreseeing that such courses must needs tend to destruction of them all, they agreed by common league to bind each other from mutual injury, and jointly defend themselves against any that gave disturbance or opposition to such agreement. Hence came Cities, Towns and Commonwealths. And because no faith in all was found sufficiently binding, they saw it needful to ordain some authority, that might restrain by force and punishment what was violated against peace and common right. This authority and power of self-defence and preservation being originally and naturally in every one of them, and unitedly in them all, for ease, for order, and lest each man should be his own partial Judge, they communicated and derived either to one, whom for the eminence of his wisdom and integrity they chose above the rest, or to more than one whom they thought of equal deserving: the first was called a King; the other Magistrates. Not to be their Lords and Masters (though afterward those names in some places were given voluntarily to such as had been authors of inestimable good to the people) but, to be their Deputies and Commissioners, to execute, by virtue of their entrusted power, that justice which else every man by the bond of nature and of Covenant must have executed for himself, and for one another.

Here is the Puritan myth of power in its political application: a demolition of the divine right of kings by means of the prior authority of divine creation and covenant, from the pen of the author of that greatest of all rewriters of the Genesis myth. Posterity knows John Milton as the poet of *Paradise Lost*, but his political influence is as epochal as that of Eusebius of Caesarea. Where Eusebius was the author of the divine right of the ruler to govern as the image of Christ on earth, Milton articulated the logic that the image of God in every human being provides a primordial precedent deeper

> than any king's authority to power on earth as well as redemption in heaven.

Cromwell's Commonwealth did not last long beyond his death, and Charles II, son of Charles I, was recalled from exile in 1660. Even so, England was not done with revolutions. James II (1685–88) attempted to impose a Catholic settlement, and leaders of Parliament negotiated with William, Prince of Orange, to take over the throne. He did that so effectively that his achievement is called the Glorious Revolution, and the Toleration Act of 1689 at last accorded British subjects the sort of religious freedom enjoyed in the Netherlands.

THE ENLIGHTENMENT

The British model of a constitutional monarchy checked by the rights and interests of its subjects spawned the Enlightenment's political theory. John Locke, in his "Two Treatises on Government" (1689) opposed any arbitrary construction of power and insisted upon the natural rights of individuals to life, liberty, and property. His argument shows a debt to John Milton, but also a growing reliance on the conception that "the people" in aggregate might be capable of exercising reason better than monarchs.

JOHN LOCKE

The Miltonian aspect of Locke's argument is evident in his citation from the opening chapters of Genesis (*First Treatise* § 145):

> The Scripture says not a word of their Rulers or Forms of Government, but only gives an account, how Mankind came to be divided into distinct Languages and Nations; and therefore 'tis not to argue from the Authority of Scripture, to tell us positively, *Fathers* were their *Rulers*, when the Scripture says no such thing, but to set up Fancies of ones own Brain, when we confidently aver Matter of Fact, where Records are utterly silent.

Although Locke's argument is formally similar to Milton's, it results in a more sweeping claim for the capacity of people to determine their own form of government, as Locke's conclusion then makes clear (*Second Treatise* § 241–43):

> But farther, this Question, (*Who shall Judge?*) cannot mean, that there is no Judge at all. For where there is no Judication on Earth, to decide Controversies amongst Men, *God* in Heaven is *Judge*; He alone, 'tis true, is Judge of the Right. But *every* Man is *Judge* for himself, as in all other Cases, so in this, whether another hath put himself into a State of War with him, and whether he should appeal to the Supreme Judge, as *Jephtha* did. If a Controversie arise between a Prince and some of the People, in a matter where the Law is silent, or doubtful, and the thing be of great Consequence, I should think the proper *Umpire*, in such a Case, should be the Body of the *People*. For in Cases where the Prince hath a Trust reposed in him, and is dispensed from the common ordinary Rules of the Law; there, if any Men find themselves aggrieved, and think the Prince acts contrary to, or beyond that Trust, who so proper to *Judge* as the Body of the *People* (who, at first, lodg'd that Trust in him) how far they meant it should extend? But if the Prince, or whoever they be in the Administration, decline that way of Determination, the Appeal then lies no where but to Heaven. Force between either Persons, who have no known Superiour on Earth, or which permits no Appeal to a Judge on Earth, being properly a state of War, wherein the Appeal lies only to Heaven, and in that State the *injured Part must judge* for himself, when he will think fit to make use of that Appeal, and put himself upon it.

Locke did not hesitate to call for a new settlement in regard to religion in order to facilitate this process of opening government and public affairs to the sway of Reason (*Letters concerning Toleration*, 1689–93):

> The toleration of those that differ from others in matters of religion, is so agreeable to the Gospel of Jesus Christ, and to the genuine reason of

mankind. ... I esteem it above all things necessary to distinguish exactly the business of civil government from that of religion, and to settle the just bound that lies between the one and the other. If this be not done, there can be no end put to the controversies that will be always arising.

In a few lines, Locke establishes the foundation for both the distinction between church and state and the inherent liberties of individuals, both keystones of the Enlightenment and of the modern age.

THE REIGN OF SCIENCE AND THE RULE OF REASON

In conditions of war and struggle, the discoveries of science seemed to offer some prospect of rational order. Pope Gregory XIII gave his name to the calendrical reform in 1582 that slightly shortened the year as counted out in days, to accord better with the solar cycle. Protestant England was loath to admit the fact, but since it was a more accurate calendar, an Act of Parliament at last promulgated it in 1752. Russia did not make the change until the Soviet Revolution, and the Orthodox Easter is still computed on the Julian calendar rather than the present Gregorian calendar. Although the Catholic Reformation is not usually associated with the Enlightenment, the simple fact of the matter is that the method of counting our days, taken increasingly as a matter of course, came from the Vatican's efforts to reassert its authority on rational grounds.

Although the papacy had been a vital force in the encouragement of science, Galileo famously proved too much of a challenge. His embrace of the Copernican theory that the earth moved around the sun seemed to contradict the dogma that humanity was the purpose and height of God's creation. Galileo was forced to recant and kept under house arrest by the Inquisition in 1633, just one year after publishing "A Dialogue Between the Two Great Systems of the World." Nonetheless, Galileo inspired René Descartes in his "Discourse on Method" (1637) to craft his method of doubting one's thoughts and perceptions. Descartes held that matter followed laws of mathematics, while the mind brought one to the Spirit of

God. Descartes lived in the Netherlands rather than his native France, to some extent wary of the kind of response Galileo had received at the hands of Catholic doctrine. But Descartes' example should long ago have put to rest the frequently repeated claim that Catholic Europe was inimical to the Enlightenment and to science.

With its claim that the methods of science can be applied to human affairs in all their range, the Enlightenment became a dominant cultural force in Europe. It was more than an intellectual fashion; it was a transnational cause. Descartes' program of explaining the material world mathematically was taken up by Sir Isaac Newton in *Mathematical Principles of Natural Philosophy* (1687). His laws of motion revolutionized the physical understanding of the universe and dominated the imagination of Europe.

Newton's rules for reasoning are economical and now recognized almost universally. These conceptions of an ordered world, accessible by observation and reason, became self-evident truths in Enlightenment Europe. Although Newton himself was actively engaged in other forms of philosophical thinking, including Hermeticism and Platonism, and at the end of his life described all his work in comparison to a child playing at the seaside, without cognizance of the vast ocean beyond, his Aristotelian and mechanical account of the cosmos was embraced throughout Europe.

With the influence of Newton's approach, the principle of reasoning from induction and inference on the basis of observation and experiment, rather than deductively from a priori principles, became standard in every field of human endeavor, including religion. Although the twentieth century saw the eclipse of Newton's views of particles (with Heisenberg's Uncertainty Principle) and of gravitation (with Einstein's General Theory of Relativity), his insistence upon induction rather than deduction in critical thinking remains dominant. "*The analogy of Nature, which is wont to be simple, and always consonant with itself*" indeed became "the foundation of all philosophy." It appeared that Nature (conceived of as a cosmic, anthropomorphic teacher) had herself healed the breach between matter and mind that Descartes had identified. Newton gave logical rigor to an almost poetic veneration of Nature, an inheritance from the Renaissance that is characteristic of the Enlightenment.

ISAAC NEWTON'S RENOWN

Alexander Pope wrote of Newton's achievement in his "An Essay on Man" (1733), but his puckish humor attests the range of Newton's influence:

> Superior beings, when of late they saw
> A mortal man unfold all Nature's law,
> Admired such wisdom in an earthly shape,
> And show'd a NEWTON as we show an ape.
> Could he, whose rules the rapid comet bind,
> Describe or fix one movement of his mind?

The very angels Newton supplanted are made to show him off in admiration. He seemed to have plumbed the mind of God.

Reason itself came to be used to frame political settlements that were more just and durable than the monarchies of the Middle Ages, the Renaissance, and the Reformation. The divine right of kings was replaced by the balance of powers among interested citizens and their inclusion in a social covenant or compact. Jean-Jacques Rousseau and Montesquieu were especially influential as theorists who built upon the insights of John Locke. The impact of their ideas in France and in Britain's American colonies proved literally revolutionary.

SUMMARY

In this chapter, we have seen how:

- The Reformation's focus on faith was rooted in medieval movements and concerns, especially in the expectation that Francis of Assisi offered a new dispensation as compared to the settled hierarchy of the Church.
- Erasmus of Rotterdam sharpened the practical edge of concerns for reform by developing an interest in the original languages of the Bible and criticizing the expense involved in the papacy.

- The construction of St Peter's in Rome, however, demanded recourse to the sale of indulgences, which provoked the deep enmity of Martin Luther.
- Jean Calvin, together with Luther, produced a systemic shift in Christianity, by putting faith in the place of the ritual requirements of the religion.
- The wars of religion which ensued saw a turn to values long cherished in the *Philokalia* of Orthodoxy, which emphasized the divine nature of human beings.
- This was an argument that John Milton applied to the political arena and John Locke developed its implications.

FURTHER READING

Bingaman, Brock and Nassif, Bradley (eds) (2012) *The Philokalia. A Classic Text of Orthodox Spirituality* (Oxford: Oxford University Press).

Chadwick, Owen (1990) *The Reformation* (London: Penguin).

Cottret, Bernard (2000) *Calvin: A Biography* (translator M. Wallace McDonald) (Grand Rapids, MI: Eerdmans).

Haile, H. G. (1980) *Luther. An Experiment in Biography* (Garden City, NY: Doubleday).

McGrath, Alister (1999) *Reformation Thought. An Introduction* (Oxford: Blackwell).

Reeves, Marjorie (1969) *The Influence of Prophecy in the Later Middle Ages. A Study in Joachimism* (Oxford: Clarendon Press).

Wandel, Lee Palmer (2011) *The Reformation. Towards a New History* (Cambridge and New York: Cambridge University Press).

5

THE BASICS OF MODERN CHRISTIANITY
CONFLICTS OF IDENTITY

The modern period opened with enthusiasm for the capacity of reason to resolve basic questions of human existence: metaphysical, scientific, and social. Over the course of time, depending upon rationality *alone* to deal with complex issues seemed simplistic. Modern thought gave way to what has been called a postmodern skepticism in regard to the efficacy of reason by itself. Christianity has been conflicted in its evaluation of the Enlightenment virtues that it was largely responsible for developing.

The conviction and the experience of the early Enlightenment were that religion and reason went hand in hand. In Catholic France, Blaise Pascal, a brilliant mathematician who died in 1662, expressed the poetic conviction that rigorous logic and the revelation of the God of Abraham, Isaac, and Jacob were complementary.

BLAISE PASCAL

To Pascal, in his posthumously published "Thoughts," the truth of Christ was demonstrable in nature and history (*Pensées* 616):

> Let us consider that, since the beginning of the world, the expectation or worship of the Messiah has subsisted without

> interruption; that there have been men who said that God had
> revealed to them that a Redeemer who would save His people
> would be born; that Abraham came afterwards to say that it had
> been revealed to him that He would be born of him by a son
> that he would have; that Jacob declared that among his twelve
> children He would be born of Judah; that Moses and the prophets
> came afterwards to announce the time and manner of His coming;
> that they said that the law which they had was valid only until
> the coming the Messiah's; that until then it would be perpetual,
> but that the other would endure forever; that thus their law, or
> that of the Messiah, of which it was a promise, would always be
> on earth; that in fact it has always lasted; that finally Jesus Christ
> came in all the foretold circumstances. That is admirable.

Secular thinkers seem never to tire of remarking on the paradox of
Pascal's faithful rationality and rational faith, but he expressed a
widespread conviction of the Enlightenment that reason and revelation
both derived from the mind of God.

Jean-Jacques Rousseau confidently brought the insight of reason
together with the sensibilities of religion, as he has a priest articulate
in his 1762 novel, *Emile, or On Education*: "That Being, whose will
is his deed, whose principle of action is in himself—that Being, in a
word, whatever it be, that gives motion to all parts of the universe,
and governs all things, I call GOD." Rousseau combined Locke's
understanding of a social contract among human beings and
between human beings with their God with Milton's numinous
sense of the primordial covenant that bound all living things together.

But some Enlightenment thinkers represented the thought that
the balance of interests that produced justice was a more compelling
truth than even the existence of God. Baron de Montesquieu, in a
letter written in 1721, articulated this growing divorce between
reason and faith that came to characterize the Enlightenment:
"Thus if there were no God, we would still be obliged to venerate
justice, that is, we should do everything possible to resemble that
being of whom we have such an exalted notion and who, if he exists,
would necessarily be just."

With no less vehemence, Jonathan Edwards of Connecticut insisted
that emotions have their role in divine revelation. Edwards understood

that reason was not merely empirical, but reached into the realm of emotions, so that a human being could stand before his Creator with integrity. Enlightenment was not a matter of arid deduction, but of a complete transformation of the thinking and believing person. Even as he made his argument, however, the Romantic movement insisted that emotions in themselves could make their own laws.

JONATHAN EDWARDS

In his *Treatise concerning Religious Affections* (1746), Jonathan Edwards set out a classic Enlightenment position:

> Holy affections are not heat without light; but evermore arise from some information of the understanding, some spiritual instruction that the mind receives, some light or actual knowledge. The child of God is graciously affected, because he sees and understands something more of divine things than he did before, more of God or Christ and of the glorious things exhibited in the gospel; he has some clearer and better view than he had before, when he was not affected; either he receives some understanding of divine things that is new to him; or has his former knowledge renewed after the view was decayed ...

> Now there are many affections which don't arise from any light in the understanding. And when it is thus, it is a sure evidence that those affections are not spiritual, let them be ever so high. Indeed they have some new apprehensions which they had not before. Such is the nature of man, that it is impossible his mind should be affected, unless it be by something that he apprehends, or that his mind conceives. But in many persons those apprehensions or conceptions that they have, wherewith they are affected, have nothing of the nature of knowledge or instruction in them. As for instance; when a person is affected with a lively idea, suddenly excited in his mind, of some shape, or very beautiful pleasant form of countenance, or some shining light, or other glorious outward appearance: here is something apprehended or conceived by the mind; but there is nothing of the nature of instruction in it: persons become never the wiser by such things, or more knowing about God, or a mediator between God and man, or the way of salvation by Christ, or

anything contained in any of the doctrines of the gospel. Persons by these external ideas have no further acquaintance with God, as to any of the attributes or perfections of his nature; nor have they any further understanding of his word, or any of his ways or works. Truly spiritual and gracious affections are not raised after this manner: they arise from the enlightening of the understanding to understand the things that are taught of God and Christ, in a new manner, the coming to a new understanding of the excellent nature of God, and his wonderful perfections, some new view of Christ in his spiritual excellencies and fullness, or things opened to him in a new manner, that appertain to the way of salvation by Christ, whereby he now sees how it is, and understands those divine and spiritual doctrines which once were foolishness to him.

THE UNRAVELING OF REASON

Edwards and Pascal, Protestant and Catholic respectively, represent the high-water mark of the Enlightenment. After them, events and inquiry turned against confidence in the harmony of reason and revelation. Reason, empirical phenomena, and emotions seemed to go their separate ways. Descartes had already observed that matter and mind were on different planes, and this divide reached within reason itself with the thought of Immanuel Kant. He believed that pure reason, reflection on phenomena, and the practical reason that leads to ethical judgments are quite different kinds of cognition.

Kant also argued that the exercise of reason was actually inhibited by religion, in a way that has influenced philosophers to this day.

IMMANUEL KANT

In his essay, "What is Enlightenment?" (1784) Immanuel Kant wrote:

If we are asked, "Do we now live in an *enlightened age*?" the answer is, "No," but we do live in an *age of enlightenment*. As things now stand, much is lacking which prevents men from being, or easily becoming, capable of correctly using their own reason in religious matters with assurance and free from outside

> direction. But, on the other hand, we have clear indications that the field has now been opened wherein men may freely deal with these things and that the obstacles to general enlightenment or the release from self-imposed tutelage are gradually being reduced. In this respect, this is the age of enlightenment, or the century of Frederick.
>
> A prince who does not find it unworthy of himself to say that he holds it to be his duty to prescribe nothing to men in religious matters but to give them complete freedom, while renouncing the haughty name of *tolerance*, is himself enlightened and deserves to be esteemed by the grateful world and posterity as the first, at least from the side of government, who divested the human race of its tutelage and left each man free to make use of his reason in matters of conscience.

Kant's confidence in the sufficiency of reason to determine the policy of the state in regard to religion is surprising in two ways. First, the role of intuition in Kant's analysis of reason, especially practical reason, might have made for a less confident assertion of reason's public capacity to correct religion. Secondly, Kant's praise of enlightened monarchy shows the extent to which his own program of Enlightenment was tied to a distinctly pro-imperial conception of authority, rather than the ideals that guided the American Revolution and were about to unleash the French Revolution five years after Kant wrote.

Imperially authorized power was necessary, in his mind, to free people from the tyranny of religion:

> For this enlightenment, however, nothing is required but freedom, and indeed the most harmless among all the things to which this term can properly be applied. It is the freedom to make public use of one's reason at every point. But I hear on all sides, "Do not argue!" The officer says: "Do not argue but drill!" The tax collector: "Do not argue but pay!" The cleric: "Do not argue but believe!"

In Kant's essay, the shift from freedom of religion to freedom from religion is achieved as if it were without effort.

Confident children of the Enlightenment such as Thomas Jefferson could likewise conceive of God as requiring no miracles to support faith in his providence. His famous colleague, Benjamin Franklin, in popular terms a more influential thinker, put this Enlightenment piety in plain language, and articulated a view of theology and of Jesus which characterizes Liberal Christianity to this day.

BENJAMIN FRANKLIN'S CREED

In a letter to the president of Yale College, Ezra Stiles, Benjamin Franklin stated shortly before his death in 1790:

Here is my creed. I believe in one God, Creator of the universe. That he governs it by his Providence. That he ought to be worshipped. That the most acceptable service we render to him is doing good to his other children. That the soul of Man is immortal, and will be treated with justice in another life respecting its conduct in this. These I take to be the fundamental principles of all sound religion, and I regard them as you do in whatever sect I meet with them.

As to Jesus of Nazareth, my opinion of whom you particularly desire, I think the system of morals and his religion, as he left them to us, the best the world ever saw or is likely to see; but I apprehend it has received various corrupting changes, and I have, with most of the present dissenters in England, some doubts as to his divinity; tho' it is a question I do not dogmatize upon, having never studied it, and think it needless to busy myself with it now, when I expect soon an opportunity of knowing the truth with less trouble.

Believers who insisted on the rational order of the universe without miraculous intervention such as Jefferson and Franklin were called "Deists," and David Hume produced an "Essay on Miracles" (1748) that is a classic of the Enlightenment during a period which saw reason and revelation going their separate ways: "A miracle is a violation of the laws of nature; and as a firm and unalterable experience has established these laws, the proof against a miracle, from the nature of the fact, is as entire as any argument from experience can possibly be imagined." The growing divide in philosophy and religion was reinforced by political turmoil. The

French Revolution unleashed its "Reign of Terror" against political enemies in the name of Reason, with Catholic priests required to convert to "the Cult of Pure Reason," or face death.

THE "REIGN OF TERROR"

The irony that reason could be deployed to justify deliberately demeaning violence surfaced during the French Revolution, and has been repeated many times thereafter. At Châlons-sur-Marne in 1794, a chronicle records:

> A detachment of cavalry, national constabulary, and hussars mingled together to strengthen the bonds of fraternity led the march, and on their pennant there were these words: "Reason guides us and enlightens us." It was followed by the company of cannoneers of Chalons, preceded by a banner with this inscription: "Death to the Tyrants." This company was followed by a cart loaded with broken chains, on which were six prisoners of war and a few wounded being cared for by a surgeon; this cart carried two banners, front and back, with these two inscriptions, "Humanity is a Republican virtue" and "They were very mistaken in fighting for tyrants."

As the French Revolution degraded itself with tactics of violence and humiliation, political theories of the Enlightenment seemed to be called into question by experience, and Napoleon Bonaparte's rise and astounding conquests pulled all of Europe into a reactionary posture of supporting the old monarchies and traditional settlements with new fervor.

The nineteenth century saw a reaction against the Enlightenment in religion as well as in politics. Churches attempted to shore up their claims of authority intellectually and legally, and professing religion became a formal requirement of attending universities in Europe. Increasingly, philosophers took refuge in the insistence that reason is worked out in the mind rather than in the world. F. D. E. Schleiermacher in Germany pioneered an idea cherished by the Romantic movement, that insight is a matter of intuition and sensibility, not deduction from observation.

F. D. E. SCHLEIERMACHER

F. D. E. Schleiermacher wrote to his future wife in 1807, to console her on her first husband's death:

> What would, or what ought to satisfy you in a future life, you cannot know; for you cannot know the order that prevails there. But when you are removed thither you will know it, and then there, as little as here, you will desire what would be opposed to it, and most assuredly it will afford you as full and rapturous satisfaction. But if your imagination suggests to you a merging in the great All, do not let this fill you with bitter anguish. Do not conceive of it as a lifeless, but as a living commingling—as the highest life. Is not the ideal toward which we are all striving even in this world, though we never reach it, the merging of the life of each in the life of all, and the putting away from us of every semblance of a separate existence? If then he lives in God, and you love him eternally in God, as you knew God and loved God in him, can you conceive of anything more glorious or more delightful? Is it not that the highest goal which love can reach, compared with which every feeling which clings to the personal life, and springs from that alone, is as nothing?

More influential than Schleiermacher over the long term, G. W. F. Hegel developed a dialectical argument to the effect that, even with its setbacks (some of which he was undoubtedly living through), the progress of history was a matter of interactions of conflicting ideas and their synthesis with what he called spirit. Indeed, Hegel described the interactions of the state and religion as crucial in this process and culminating in a single uniting power.

G. W. F. HEGEL

Hegel even argued that the end of freedom would ultimately reveal that the state and religion are not separate after all ("The Relationship of Religion to the State," 1831):

> The state is the true mode of actuality; in it, the true ethical will attains actuality and the spirit lives in its true form. Religion is

divine knowledge, the knowledge which human beings have of God and of themselves in God. This is divine wisdom and the field of absolute truth. But there is a second wisdom, the wisdom of the world, and the question arises as to its relationship to the former, divine wisdom.

In general, religion and the foundation of the state are one and the same thing—they are *identical in and for themselves*. In the patriarchal condition and the Jewish theocracy, the two are not yet distinct and are still outwardly identical. Nevertheless, the two are also different, and in due course, they become strictly separated from each other; but then they are once more posited as genuinely identical. That the two have then attained that unity which has being in and for itself follows from what has been said; religion is knowledge of the highest truth, and this truth, defined more precisely, is *free spirit*. In religion, human beings are free before God. In making their will conform to the divine will, they are not opposed to the divine will but have themselves within it; they are free inasmuch as they have succeeded, in the religious cult, in overcoming the division. The state is merely *freedom in the world*, in actuality. The essential concept here is that concept of freedom which a people carries in its self-consciousness, for the concept of freedom is realized in the state, and an essential aspect of this realization is the consciousness of freedom with being in and for itself. Peoples who do not know that human beings are free in and for themselves live in a benighted state both with regard to their constitution and to their religion.—There is *one* concept of freedom in both religion and the state. This *one* concept is the highest thing which human beings have, and it is realized by them. A people which has a bad concept of God also has a bad state, a bad government, and bad laws.

Karl Marx attempted to work out Hegel's system in political and economic terms. Marx's own orientation was not totalitarian, but his development of Hegel's idealism would contribute to the command and control states of the twentieth century. That was not because Marx or Hegel favored a return to divine right as a model of authority, but because they saw the powers of human community flowing into a union of power.

KARL MARX

The young Marx wrote in 1842 on the plight of peasants in the Mosel region:

> Therefore, to resolve the difficulty, the administration and the people administered both equally need a *third* element, which is *political* without being official and hence does not proceed from bureaucratic premises, an element which is likewise *civil* without being directly involved in private interests and their needs. This supplementary element which *bears the mind of a citizen concerned with the state* and *the heart of one concerned with civil society* is the free press.

The European revolutions of 1848, partially encouraged by Marx's thought but pushed forward by famine and fierce pressures for democracy, exacerbated the sense that a dedication to reason was unleashing forces of chaos, and the American Civil War confirmed that impression. Finally, however, two intellectual developments—evolution in science and history in the humanities—ensured that reason and revelation would no longer be seen as complementary, despite Hegel's attempt to finesse a hybrid with his conception of freedom ensconced in power.

With the publication of Charles Darwin's *On the Origin of Species* in 1859, evolution seemed to provide an elegant account of the taxonomy of living beings, without reference to God.

CHARLES DARWIN'S *ON THE ORIGIN OF SPECIES*

Darwin's theory seemed to him compatible with his Deist theology, as he wrote at the close of *On the Origin of Species*:

> Thus from the war of nature, from famine and death, the most exalted object which we are capable of conceiving, namely, the

production of higher animals, directly follows. There is a grandeur in this view of life, with its several powers, having been originally breathed into a few forms or into one; and that, whilst this planet has gone cycling on according to the fixed law of gravity, from so simple a beginning endless forms most beautiful and most wonderful have been, and are being, evolved.

In 1863 the publication of Ernest Renan's *Vie de Jésus* revolutionized the study of Jesus and marks the moment when the Enlightenment's compromise between faith and rationality came to be seen as historically untenable.

ERNEST RENAN'S *VIE DE JÉSUS*

Renan believed that Jesus could be appreciated—and could only be appreciated—as evolved in historical terms, apart from dogma:

Jesus, it is seen, never in his action went out of the Jewish circle. Although his sympathy for all the despised of orthodoxy led him to admit the heathen into the kingdom of God, although he had more than once resided in a pagan country, and once or twice he is found in kindly relations with unbelievers, it may be said that his life was passed entirely in the little world, close and narrow as it was, in which he was born. The Greek and Roman countries heard nothing of him; his name does not figure in profane authors until a hundred years later, and then only indirectly, in connection with seditious movements provoked by his doctrine, or persecutions of which his disciples were the object. Within the heart even of Judaism, Jesus did not make any durable impression. Philo, who died about the year 50, has no glimpse of him. Josephus, born in the year 37, and writing in the last years of the century, mentions his execution in a few lines, as an event of secondary importance; and in the enumeration of the sects of his time, he omits the Christians. The *Mischna*, again, presents no trace of the new school; the

> passages in the two Gemaras in which the founder of Chris-
> tianity is named, do not carry us back beyond the fourth or fifth
> century. The essential work of Jesus was the creation around
> him of a circle of disciples in whom he inspired a boundless
> attachment, and in whose breast he implanted the germ of his
> doctrine. To have made himself beloved, so much that after his
> death they did not cease to love him, this was the crowning
> work of Jesus, and that which most impressed his con-
> temporaries. His doctrine was so little dogmatical, that he never
> thought of writing it or having it written. A man became his
> disciple, not by believing this or that, but by following
> and loving him. A few sentences treasured up in the memory,
> and above all, his moral type, and the impression which he had
> produced, were all that remained of him. Jesus is not a founder
> of dogmas, a maker of symbols; he is the world's initiator of a
> new spirit.

Darwin's science refuted the picture of creation in the book of
Genesis, and Renan's history refuted any deification of Jesus. When
science and history asserted they could overthrow religion, religion
reacted, and the post-Enlightenment age (today called Postmodernism)
was born.

AUTHORITY

The simple rejection of reason, in order to assert the superiority of
faith, might have been defended on the basis of the system of
Christianity that had emerged as a result of the Reformation. In
fact, however, the assertion of authority in order to respond to the
challenge of scientific and historical empiricism incorporated reason,
rather than attempting to refute it. The claim emerged that certain
fundamentals or axioms were necessary for reason to function in the
first place. The challenges of history and science, it was argued, could
be met on that basis.

Among both Catholics and Protestants, the reaction against these
two challenges was to insist upon certain fundamentals as literally
true. In 1870, the First Vatican Council promulgated the doctrine
of papal infallibility.

THE IMMACULATE CONCEPTION

In 1854, Pope Pius IX declared the doctrine of the Immaculate Conception. This teaching does not relate directly to Jesus. The view that he was born of Mary without her having sexual intercourse is called the Virgin Birth, not the Immaculate Conception. The Immaculate Conception refers to Mary and holds that she was born without the sin that adheres to humanity as a whole. This view builds on an ancient Orthodox belief that, because Jesus was God as well as man, Mary became the *theotokos*, the God-bearer. For her to be accorded that honor, she must have been conceived without sin.

Nothing in the New Testament refers to Mary's status in these terms; they are all later developments, beginning in the second century of the Common Era. But they became a signal element in medieval piety, when Mary's Immaculate Conception contrasted sharply with the general sin into which humanity had fallen.

Fifteen years after he declared this doctrine, Pope Pius asked the first Vatican Council (1869–70) that his teaching in this regard be considered infallible. The argument was that the Church, speaking from faith, does not err, and that the pope, articulating the Church's teaching, is also not subject to error. In other words, papal infallibility is not a blanket statement that no pope ever makes a mistake, but a calibrated assertion of the authority of the Church as vested in the pope.

Coming as it did after the curtailment of papal power over territory in Italy, as nationalism there grew, the doctrine of Infallibility provided a field in which the power of the pope could be focused. After the Second World War, the synergy between the veneration of Mary and the papacy came to expression again, when in 1950 Pope Pius XII declared infallibly that the mother of Jesus was assumed into heaven at the time of her death. This doctrine is known as the Assumption of the Blessed Virgin Mary. Like the Immaculate Conception, some version of the belief had been embraced for centuries, but its explicit formulation strengthened claims of papal authority.

Among Protestants, the name of Fundamentalism was embraced, in order to insist that the Scriptures themselves set the infallible standard of faith.

THE FUNDAMENTALS OF FUNDAMENTALISM

Five main tenets were held to be "essential and necessary" teachings by the Presbyterian General Assembly in 1910. These came to be known as the Fundamentals of the Faith:

- Biblical "inerrancy" in its reflection of truth
- Birth of Jesus from a biological virgin
- Jesus' performance of miracles that defy natural law
- Jesus' atonement for the sins of others by shedding his blood on the cross
- Jesus' resurrection in the same body in which he died, and his return to earth in that body at the end of days.

During the nineteenth century and the first half of the twentieth century, resistance to the teaching of literal fundamentals was adamantly maintained among Catholics and Protestants. In France and England, those who used historical tools to assert a symbolic and evolutionary approach to interpretation were called Modernists. The most famous of them was Alfred Loisy, a French priest who found it perfectly natural to deny the infallibility of any human being, who doubted the Virgin birth of Jesus, saw Jesus' miracles as symbols, did not believe God needed a payment in blood in order to love us, and overtly denied resurrection in the same body. For him, the meaning of the Gospels resided in their capacity to transform the nature of our collective existence.

The Protestant Walter Rauschenbusch espoused a similarly collective, but less academic, theology in New York City. He called his message "the Social Gospel," and by it he intended to insist that the purpose of the Gospels was to overturn the structures of capitalism and totally to change the nature of our social life in the interests of justice.

These theologians were both praised and attacked for their symbolic, evolutionary brands of Christianity. The Vatican banned Loisy's books; he himself submitted to their banning and agreed not to engage in publication. But he refused to say that his opinions were wrong, and was excommunicated from the Catholic Church by Pope Pius X in 1908. His isolation from the Church provided him with a new opportunity: a position in the Collège de France. Rauschenbusch was Baptist pastor in Brooklyn during the final years of the century, just as Fundamentalism was making itself felt; he found a warmer welcome at the Rochester Theological Seminary, where he taught from 1897. His claim that Christianity was a matter of programmatic social action, rather than individual belief, found more support among intellectuals than in the Baptist hierarchy.

Both these thinkers are influential today. Loisy's methods, and his claims, for example, that Moses did not write the Pentateuch and that the Apostle John did not author the Gospel named after him, are now taught as standard in Catholic and Protestant seminaries. Similarly, part of the formation of any pastor—Protestant, Catholic, or (come to that) Jewish—will routinely include training in what most people would call social work and what Rauschenbusch saw as part of the gospel: counseling, community organizing, mediation, and the like. In religious academies, Loisy and Rauschenbusch prevailed a long time ago, and their approach is generally known under the name of Liberal theology.

But the popular scene has evidenced a reaction against symbol and evolution as providing keys to assessing the Gospels. Overtly Fundamentalist forms of Protestantism and papalist forms of Catholicism have enjoyed enormous growth in the United States since World War II. That is one reason why those interested in religion today have little choice but to deal with the claim of literal fundamentals in Christianity.

The symbolic and evolutionary approach of Loisy and Rauschenbusch has nonetheless persisted. It has prospered better in Europe than in America, even in popular culture. Catholic Europe has largely made its peace with papal infallibility by restricting its validity to symbolic truth. Insofar as Protestantism there is Fundamentalist at all, it is largely as a result of American influence, especially via cable television. Because American academics still tend to look to Europe as an example, it is perhaps not surprising that their academies and seminaries espouse a Liberal theology which is rarely spoken to the public at large, but which would be at home in Europe.

From that European perspective, it is a fairly easy step to confusing Fundamentalism with a devotion to literal history. From the vantage point of an emphasis upon symbol and evolution, the assertion of basic categories of revelation looks remarkably like an unsophisticated literalism. But Fundamentalism and literalism are in fact quite different.

PREDICTIONS OF CATASTROPHE

The element of Fundamentalism that has most caught popular awareness is not at all a literal application of the Bible, but a relatively recent belief in the end of the world. The focus of this belief is called "the rapture."

THE RAPTURE

During the seventeenth century, Puritan theologians in England developed an apocalyptic reading of the Bible, in which the Revelation became the lens through which other Scriptures were read. In this way, St. Paul's reference to how believers would meet with Christ in his second coming was spliced into the description of the moment of resurrection and the millennium in Revelation 20:4–5. Paul speaks of living believers who have survived those who have already died and promises that they will be united to meet Jesus as their Lord:

> This we say by a word of the Lord, that we who are alive, remaining until the *parousia* of the Lord, will not precede those who have slept. Because the Lord himself by a command, with the sound of an archangel and with God's trumpet, will descend from heaven, and the dead in Christ will arise first, then we who are alive, remaining, will be snatched up together with them in clouds to meet the Lord in the air, and so will we always be with the Lord. So reassure one another with these words.
>
> (1 Thessalonians 4:15–18)

Puritan circles conceived of the "rapture" (as the reference in 1 Thessalonians came to be called), the millennium of the Apocalypse, and the second coming (*parousia*) of Christ as all combined in a single moment of divine judgment.

While Paul's "rapture" was to be joyous, like most ancient Christian expectation of the apocalypse, the Puritan version focused more on the judgment of those who were not taken up to heaven. This change of emphasis proved fateful over the following centuries.

The New England Puritan ministers Increase Mather (1639–1723) and his son Cotton Mather (1663–1728) portrayed the saints as being taken up into the air in order to avoid the carnage left behind on the earth. Those "left behind" after the rapture faced hell on earth, a scenario that came to be reinforced over time. This became the classic pre-millenialist view, according to which Christ's second coming needed to happen before the millennium could begin. It contrasted to the post-millenialist perspective—with its emphasis on the progress through the millennium until the second coming—under the influence of thinkers such as Isaac Newton and Jonathan Edwards.

The pre-millenialist perspective was greatly strengthened and popularized by the rise of Dispensationalism, which conceived of human history and experience as developing through distinct covenants or Dispensations until the final judgment.

DISPENSATIONALISM

The Anglo-Irish priest John Nelson Darby (1800–82) pursued a pre-millenarian reading of 1 Thessalonians 4:17 within an apocalyptic scenario inspired by the Revelation. He did so without specifying a date. In the 1830s he developed his teaching of the rapture as an instantaneous but unpredictable event. Relying heavily on the "rapture" passage (1 Thessalonians 4:17) and its pairing with the book of Revelation, Darby added an innovation: the prediction of seven years of tribulation at the hands of the antichrist for those who remained on earth. They run the gauntlet of tribulation and are subjected to the thousand-year rule of the saints after the war named after Armageddon in Revelation 16:14–16. All that is only preliminary to final judgment. This comprehensive expectation and its avoidance of precise prediction made Darby's views attractive in America both during his life and long after. Only an abrupt shift in the ages could bring the dawn of Christ's kingdom in the growing conviction of many Christians. Darby's single-mindedness and dedicated preaching far and wide led to the rapid spread of this pre-millenarian religious yearning. His theology of "dispensations," successive epochs of God's relationship to humanity, became widespread. They included the seven generations of Adam, Noah, Abraham, Israel, the Gentiles, the Church, and—finally—the millennium, the last initiated by the rapture and completing the sequence of seven established in the Apocalypse. The content of the dispensations derives from the Bible as a whole, but their number and the means by which one leads to another were spelled out, in Darby's view, in the Revelation of John.

Darby pre-dated the emergence of twentieth-century Fundamentalism, but the rise of the modern Fundamentalist movement provided a boost to his theology. He read the Bible—as later Fundamentalists wished to—as an inerrant whole. Putting 1 Thessalonians and the Revelation together was from this point of view not an anachronism, but a faithful assertion that the Scripture forms a seamless whole. A single publication supported both Dispensationalism and Fundamentalism during their extraordinary advance in America during the twentieth century. In 1909 Cyrus Scofield first published his Reference Bible with Oxford University Press; the book consisted of the King James Version with Dispensationalist notes and eventually a chronology that included Archbishop Ussher's dating of creation to 4004 BCE. Presented as part of an already widely cherished translation of the Bible, Dispensationalism and Fundamentalism both appeared to be traditional forms of Christianity.

Seismic events in the history of the twentieth century favored the rise of Dispensationalist Fundamentalism. World War I gave the lie to the idea of the steady progress of Western civilization and particularly to idealistic views of the efficacy of government. And how could you deride what Walter Rauschenbusch tried to dismiss as "faith in catastrophes," when catastrophic events, quickly and fully reported by an unprecedented increase of mass communication from the turn of the last century onward, became routine news in the experience of virtually everyone in the developed world?

Scofield scoffed at the idea of any form of progressive evolution. He so abhorred the myth of progress that he even held—detailing his comment in exposition on 2 Thessalonians 2:3—that "the predicted future of the visible church is apostasy." People in themselves are not perfectible, and their attempts at perfection bring only corruption. Most Christians would be left behind while only true believers were raptured. When leaders such as Rauschenbusch criticized his theology or his personal life, Scofield portrayed them to be agents of Satan "transformed as the ministers of righteousness."

In the tradition of pre-millenialist prophecy during the nineteenth century, Scofield had predicted the Jews' return to Palestine and portrayed the apocalyptic "Gog" (Revelation 20:8) as Russia. At the dawn of the twentieth century, these seemed distant events to most observers and improbable to many. But then came the aftermath of the twentieth century's second calamitous world war, with the establishment of the State of Israel in 1948 and the start of the Cold War—in which the Soviet Union emerged as the major antagonist of the United States. These events became irresistible signs for some of God's impending and definitive intervention in the rapture, the tribulation, and the millennium.

The stage was set for a new dispensation and a fusing of Christian Fundamentalism with American patriotism. Books such as Hal Lindsey's *The Late, Great Planet Earth* encouraged the expectation of an imminent pre-millennial return of Christ and the start of a new millennium very, very soon. The calendars and exact predictions varied, of course, from writer to writer, but their specificity meant that Darby's reticence about calculating the time of the end was definitively left behind.

THE "LEFT BEHIND" SERIES

The best-known Dispensationalist predictions about Jerusalem in recent times have come from the phenomenally successful author of apocalyptic fiction, Tim LaHaye (with Jerry B. Jenkins). Creator of the best-selling Left Behind series of the 1990s and 2000s, LaHaye portrays the Revelation of John as a forecast of how a new temple must be built in Jerusalem in order to provoke a war that will bring human civilization to an end before Jesus' return in glory.

The elaborate scenario imagined by LaHaye in his novels—adapted in a series of successful feature films—resolves a long-standing problem experienced by those who hold literally to apocalyptic readings of the New Testament. In the Synoptic Gospels Jesus appears to predict the destruction of the Temple in Jerusalem and the subsequent coming of the cosmic Son of Man to judge all humanity (Matt 24–25; Mark 13; Luke 21). But while the Romans did indeed burn down Jerusalem and its temple in 70 CE, no judgment by the Son of Man followed. Why did the judgment not come if, as Fundamentalists believe, Scripture is infallible and if Jesus' prophecy were valid?

LaHaye sets out as the cornerstone of his work that Jesus actually referred to the destruction of a *Third* Temple to be built in the future. (The temple destroyed by the Romans was the Second Temple, which had been erected by Jews returning to their homeland after a long period of exile in Babylon. That exile had begun after the destruction of the First Jewish Temple in 586 BCE.) When that Third Temple is destroyed, the end will be truly upon us, for in the apocalyptic new Jerusalem there is no sacrificial temple left at all: "the Lord God, the Almighty, is the temple, and the Lamb" (Revelation 21:22).

This is all part of the new heaven and new earth promised in the Apocalypse (21:1), which presupposes comprehensive and cosmic destruction during the course of divine judgment and culminates in Jesus' coming as the Word of God described two chapters earlier (19:11–13). That cosmic disaster, also anticipated in the Synoptic Gospels, simply did not occur with the Roman arson of the Temple in 70 CE. By resetting the apocalyptic clock of both the Revelation of John and the Synoptic Gospels to the erection of a Third Temple, their eschatological scenarios could be maintained.

Even as Protestant Christianity developed a sharp-edged eschatology on the basis of the Revelation of John, Roman Catholicism pursued a reading of that text that insisted on its eternal significance. The celestial woman who is portrayed in Revelation 12 was identified as the Blessed Virgin Mary, whose bodily assumption into heaven was declared by Pope Pius XII as infallible doctrine in 1950.

THE ROSARY

Prayer beads are part of the meditative practice of most major religions. They enable practitioners to keep track of the cycle of contemplation that they follow, while devoting their primary attention to prayer in itself. Roman Catholicism has systematized the use of such beads in the Rosary, a precisely sequenced cycle of the "Mysteries" of Christ, from the announcement of his birth (the Annunciation) to his ascension and Mary's assumption. These are called the "Joyful," "Sorrowful," and "Glorious" Mysteries. In 2002, Pope John Paul II added a sequence of "Luminous" Mysteries. In the Rosary, alongside the Paternoster, the "Angelus," is said: "Hail Mary, full of grace, the Lord is with thee; blessed art thou amongst women, and blessed is the fruit of thy womb, Jesus. Pray for us sinners now and in the hour of our death." Although the first part of this prayer derives from the New Testament (Luke 1:28, 42), its substance derives from much more recent adoration of Mary.

Where, in theology, Fundamentalism, Liberal interpretation, and Papal Catholicism collided, all of them ideologically committed and decreasingly historical in their basic orientation, in literary discussion, structuralism and deconstruction vied for influence. Structuralism posited that in the development of language and literature, certain essentials of discourse could be discerned and that, without such discernment, interpretation was impossible. Deconstruction, in contrast, insisted that meaning only occurs in the mind of the interpreter, by means of engagement with the text (and sometimes without that benefit, in theoretical discussion which non-Deconstructionists often find difficult or impossible to follow).

ECUMENISM

Although theology in the late twentieth century shied away from history, history did not retreat from theology. The basic facts of the Holocaust, emerging out of Christianity's post-Enlightenment crisis, and of militant Islam, a direct consequence of Christian policies of war and oppression, have rooted Christian thought afresh in historical contingency. Dialogue with Judaism has proceeded vigorously, and the inclusion of Islam within comparative theology has become standard.

In the Roman Catholic Church, a sign of what openness to new historical expressions of faith can mean was shown by the pontificate of Angelo Roncalli, better known as Pope John XXIII—the greatest reformer in the modern history of Roman Catholicism. Soon after his election in 1958, he called the Second Vatican Council, making it clear that he wished the work of renewal to be undertaken by the bishops assembled, rather than by the court of the pope himself. Despite opposition, the Council opened in 1962, and when that first session closed John announced himself satisfied with the work of updating (*aggiornamento*). He convened the second session for the following year, but he died of cancer on 3 June 1963, before that session convened.

Despite the brevity of his pontificate and continuing disputes concerning the meaning of Vatican II, in one regard there can be no question of the impact of John XXIII. The Council accepted that the Mass and other sacraments should be made available in the actual language of the people who participated, rather than in Latin. Moreover, the report on liturgy also allowed that local variation, rather than rigid uniformity, should be admitted and encouraged in the development of worship. Both those principles, associated with Protestantism since the sixteenth century, entered the Catholic tradition with John's endorsement.

In this case, the rule of faith, which had long been discussed by Catholic theologians and pastors and laypeople, was able to articulate itself afresh in new circumstances by means of papal encouragement. The purpose, of course, was not in any way to diminish "the divine Eucharistic sacrifice," but to make it even more vivid as "the outstanding means by which the faithful can express in their lives, and manifest to others, the mystery of Christ and the real nature of the true Church." In this very clear statement, the Council made it explicit that it was not adopting a Protestant emphasis upon the individual's understanding of the faith, but was enhancing its dedication to a sacramental definition of the Church.

The same period also saw a fresh historical engagement on the part of Protestant Christianity. The Rev. Dr. Martin Luther King, Jr. set out the fundamental position behind his teaching of non-violence.

MARTIN LUTHER KING'S "LETTER FROM BIRMINGHAM JAIL"

In his "Letter from Birmingham Jail," where he was held for his opposition to laws of racial segregation, King wrote:

> One has not only a legal but a moral responsibility to obey just laws. Conversely, one has a moral responsibility to disobey unjust laws. I would agree with St. Augustine that "an unjust law is no law at all."

That brave and lucid policy is grounded in the teaching of Jesus, perhaps best expressed in the following advice (Matthew 5:38–42):

> You have heard that it was said, An eye for an eye and a tooth for a tooth. But I say to you not to resist the evil one. But to someone who strikes you on the right cheek, turn also the other. And to one who wants to enter judgment with you to take your shirt, give your cloak, too! And with someone who compels a mile's journey from you, travel with him two. Give to the one who asks of you, and do not turn away from one who wants to borrow from you.

Of all the teachings of Jesus, none is more straightforward, and none more challenging. Evil is to be overcome by means of what is usually called non-resistance.

What follows in Matthew states the principle of Jesus' teaching, that we are to love in the way that God does (Matthew 5:43–48, see Luke 6:36). The fundamental quality of that teaching in Christianity is unquestionable (see Matthew 22:34–40; Mark 12:28–34; Luke 10:25–28; Romans 13:8–10).

But in the teaching about turning the other cheek, giving the cloak, going the extra mile, offering the money, everything comes down to particular conditions that prevailed during the Roman occupation of the Near East. The fact that this formulation only appears in Matthew (written around 80 CE) has given rise to the legitimate question of whether it should be attributed to Jesus in its present form. The imagery corresponds to the conditions of the Roman occupation in an urban area, where a soldier of the empire might well demand provisions and service and money, and all with the threat of force. But even if we acknowledge (as seems only reasonable) that Matthew's Gospel has pitched Jesus' policy in the idiom of its own experience, the policy itself should be attributed to Jesus.

Why should what is usually called non-resistance to evil be recommended? It needs to be stressed that non-resistance is not the same as acquiescence. The injustice that is done is never accepted as if it were just. The acts of turning the other cheek, giving the cloak, going the additional mile, offering the money, are all designed to be excessive, so that the fact of the injustice of what is demanded is underlined. Indeed, it is not really accurate to call the behavior "non-resistance." The point is for the person who makes demands that are unjust to realize they are unjust. Just that policy served Christians and their faith well during the centuries of persecution under the Roman Empire. It was effective because it brought about an awareness within the empire, even among the enemies of Christianity, that the policy of violent persecution was unjust (and, for that matter, ineffective). Rather than a teaching of non-resistance, this is a version of the advice of how to retaliate. Instead of an eye for an eye, it suggests a cheek after a cheek. This is not non-resistance; it is exemplary response. That is, it is a form of retaliation: not to harm, but to show another way.

Christianity, with its durable and protean theology, has proven a volatile faith for two millennia and shows no sign of converting from that character. The resources of its own tradition and the influences of Islam and Judaism will probably continue to prove seminal. Equally important—and perhaps transformative for Christianity in the West—the revival of Orthodoxy in lands formerly controlled by the Soviet Union means that an entirely different view of theology, of at least equal authority and integrity, will challenge both Catholic and Protestant thinkers.

As discussion and controversy have proceeded, a fresh system has emerged, in which Christ has been seen as the meaning of the whole more than in other periods. Should we speak of Christ and Jesus as exactly the same? Is he to be seen in historical or symbolic terms? The rituals to be followed by Christians have increasingly been determined by particular communities: churches are called "denominations," on the understanding that they will determine particular practices that are to be followed. Beyond the denominations, the degree of congregational autonomy has grown to a point greater than in most periods of the history of the Church. Finally, the ethical dimension of the system has focused on the capacity of individuals to live in accord with the meaning and rituals that are espoused.

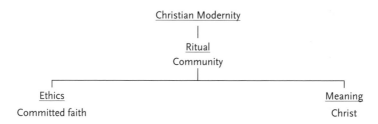

The recent iteration of the Christian system owes an unexpected debt to the thinking of Orthodoxy, especially in the shape of the thought of Fyodor Dostoevsky. Despite imprisonment for beliefs some circles in Czarist Russia considered socialist, Dostoevsky held to the view that a people's attachment to their soil (their *pochva*) implied an organic ethos of self-sacrifice and mutual love that could provide the practical and ethical guidance they required. In his novel *The Brothers Karamazov*, Dostoevsky contrasted the dedication to the soil of his hero, Alyosha, with the centralized cynical "Grand Inquisitor" of the West, who demanded that people give up the very freedom that made them a distinctive part of God's creation.

Dostoevsky's commitment to change could be described as from the bottom up, from soil to people to society to government. This dynamic was embraced in Latin America in the movement that came to call itself Liberation Theology. Speaking from a deep experience of that context, the Peruvian priest Gustavo Gutiérrez in 1970 summed up the sense of frustration at oppression in "the only continent of underdeveloped and oppressed peoples who are in a majority Christians." The long preeminence of the Roman Catholic Church there in his mind meant that theology needed to face up to the relationship between committed faith and power.

LIBERATION THEOLOGY

In "Notes for a Theology of Liberation," *Theological Studies* 31 (1970) Gutiérrez set out the agenda of a larger movement that had been emerging for nearly twenty years:

> In these pages we are particularly sensitive to the critical function of theology regarding the Church's presence and activity in the world. The principal fact about that presence today, especially in underdeveloped countries, is the participation by Christians in the struggle to construct a just and fraternal society in which men can live in dignity and be masters of their own destinies. We think that the word "development" does not well express those profound aspirations. "Liberation" seems more exact and richer in overtones; besides, it opens up a more fertile field for theological reflection.

The problem of "development" is not only its alienating privilege of profit over people, but the larger frame of how human progress should be measured:

> Liberation, therefore, seems to express better both the hopes of oppressed peoples and the fulness of a view in which man is seen not as a passive element, but as agent of history. More profoundly, to see history as a process of man's liberation places the issue of desired social changes in a dynamic context. It also permits us to understand better the age we live in. Finally, the term "development" clouds up somewhat the theological issues latent in the process. To speak of liberation, on

> the other hand, is to hint at the biblical sources that illuminate
> man's presence and actions in history: the liberation from sin
> by Christ our Redeemer and the bringing of new life.

The judgment that poverty is a function, not merely of neutral economic forces, but of sin, implies that resistance is an ethical requirement. When Gutiérrez names the enemy, he anticipates much of the language that has challenged globalization in recent decades:

> The dynamics of capitalistic economics lead simultaneously to the creation of greater wealth for fewer, and of greater poverty for more. Our national oligarchies, teamed up in complicity with these centers of power, perpetuate, for their own benefit and through various subterfuges, a situation of domination within each country.

Social revolution therefore has appeared to be an imperative to Liberation Theology, and its adherents have acknowledged that the hope of class struggle bringing about permanent change implies a debt to Marxist thought. As they see the matter, however, the postcolonial situation throughout the world has meant that oligarchy finds itself confronted with the process of liberation, sometimes in violent terms. But the emphasis on the agency of the oppressed themselves focuses attention on the establishment of "base communities," places of local religious and economic solidarity, rather than any centralized authority. The aim is nothing less than a "new man" served by a "new Christianity" that realizes its eschatological aim. Only this goal, in the view of theologians of Liberation, will do justice to the message of the Prophets in the Hebrew Bible and Jesus' preference for the poor.

Latin American bishops sometimes expressed agreement with the aims of Liberation Theology, but a considerable number preferred a less activist emphasis on doctrine. One of them was Óscar Romero, who became archbishop of San Salvador in 1977. Even by that time, however, Romero had come into contact in his ministry with workers who were targeted with violence in their efforts to organize. He wrote in a pastoral letter:

It saddens and concerns us to see the selfishness with which means and dispositions are found to nullify the just wage of the harvesters. How we would wish that the joy of this rain of rubies and all the harvests of the earth would not be darkened by the tragic sentence of the Bible: "Behold, the day wage of laborers that cut your fields defrauded by you is crying out, and the cries of the reapers have reached the ears of the Lord (James 5:4)."

The recourse of the government of El Salvador to death squads, which targeted some of Archbishop Romero's own clergy and staff, brought him into overt opposition with the authorities. He called on President Jimmy Carter to end United States aid to the government. In a radio broadcast on March 24, 1980 he called on soldiers in the National Guard to refuse to kill, saying much as Martin Luther King had that "No soldier is obliged to obey an order contrary to the law of God. No one has to obey an immoral law." Later that day, while saying Mass he was shot and killed by a paid assassin.

Romero's assassination, essentially as a martyr, prompted the demand—articulated by Leonardo Boff, a Brazilian priest—that the Church should side definitively with the poor rather than the privileged. Boff insisted in a series of essays:

There are powerful and living forces, particularly at the grassroots, that are not sufficiently recognized by the traditional channels of the church's present organization. The grassroots are asking for a new structure, a new ecclesial division of labour and of religious power, for this a new vision of the church is necessary.

But in 1985, the Congregation of the Doctrine of the Faith found that Boff's allegedly relativistic views "endanger the sound doctrine of the faith," and he was put under a discipline of silence for one year. The prefect of the Congregation, whose decision was approved by Pope John Paul II, was Joseph Ratzinger, who later became Pope Benedict XVI.

Yet the principles of Liberation Theology have exerted an influence outside Latin America, not least in the struggle in South Africa against apartheid. In 1980, the World Council of Churches (WCC) convened a conference on mission and evangelism which endorsed the principal tenets of Liberation, and they have been incorporated in the purpose of the WCC ever since. Even at the time of its founding in 1948, the robust Ecumenical agenda of the WCC brought conflict with some Protestant denominations, although the organization grew out of Protestant ecumenism, and Roman Catholic participation has been tentative. Tensions have grown over the issue of Liberation Theology, but that is only one of an array of controversies—including birth control, abortion, euthanasia, the ordination of women, the evaluation of homosexuality, and the place of human rights—that have divided churches as much within themselves as from one another.

SUMMARY

In this chapter we have seen Christianity respond to several new movements, including:

- The conception that reason alone should guide belief and behavior;
- The claims of Fundamentalism and Papal Infallibility;
- The direct challenge to the supremacy of reason with the appeal to apocalyptic intervention;
- The continuing influence of Liberal Theology, especially as it has developed into Liberation Theology.

Fragmentation over these and other issues has not only put the Ecumenical movement in question, but has also raised the question of the coherence of Christianity.

FURTHER READING

Abbott, W. M. (ed.) (1966) *The Documents of Vatican II* (New York: Guild).

Boff, Leonardo (2000) *Holy Trinity, Perfect Community* (translator Phillip Berryman) (New York: Orbis).

Chilton, Bruce (2013) *Visions of the Apocalypse. Receptions of John's Revelation in Western Imagination* (Waco, TX: Baylor University Press).

Gutiérrez, Gustavo (1988) *A Theology of Liberation. History, Politics, and Salvation* (translators Sister Caridad Inda and John Eagleson) (Maryknoll: Orbis).

Neusner, Jacob (ed.) (2006) *Religious Foundations of Western Civilization: Judaism, Christianity, and Islam* (Nashville, TN: Abingdon).

Oates, Stephen B. (1982) *Let the Trumpet Sound: The Life of Martin Luther King, Jr.* (New York: Harper and Row).

Pagden, Anthony (2013) *The Enlightenment and Why it still Matters* (Oxford: Oxford University Press).

POSTLUDES

Christianity's resilience derives from the strength of the systems we have encountered in this volume, each with its account of the rituals, ethics, and meaning that support and promote human existence. Because these systems have changed over time, a previous system can re-emerge at virtually any moment, invigorating the faith in new and unexpected ways.

Until recently, Western accounts of Christian history assumed that the Jesuit mission in the seventeenth century introduced Christianity to China in the sixteenth century. There can be no doubt about the influence and persistence of that effort. Roman Catholicism in its modern form is clearly apparent in the struggle between the Vatican and authorities in the People's Republic of China over the appointment of bishops. The system of Roman Catholicism privileges the ritual importance of hierarchy (see Chapter 4):

That emphasis directly contradicts the ritual claims of the Communist Party of China to guide a unitary state. Similarly, the official atheism of the Party set it at odds periodically with a Protestant insistence on the centrality of faith (also detailed in Chapter 4) that has made its way in China since the nineteenth century:

But a Eurocentric view of Chinese history has proven inadequate. A stone inscription from the eighth century, written in both Chinese and Syriac, reveals that in the seventh century, the emperor Taizong of the Tang dynasty endorsed what was called "the Religion of Light" (*Jingjao*). Although this form of Syriac Christianity fell victim to dynastic politics, the Orthodoxy it represents was reinforced by the introduction of Russian forms of that faith from the eighteenth century. Together with Roman Catholic and Protestant systems, then, Chinese Christianity has also been influenced by the Orthodox system in varying forms (see Chapter 2):

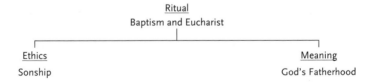

The prevalence of one system over another obviously cannot be predicted, but the growth of Christianity in China as the fastest-growing minority religion suggests that a phase of interaction among systems and consequent mutation is a likely outcome. That is especially the case, since the present modern system has emphasized a harmonious relationship among Christians:

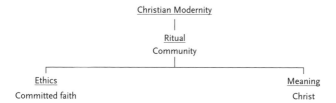

The Religion of Light represents an anticipation of this model, since it incorporated many elements of Confucian philosophy, especially its emphasis on filial piety. Chinese Christianity may well expand in the current century in the way that African Christianity did in the twentieth century.

The way in which the various systems of Christianity can influence one another helps us to address a question that arises from the present approach. If we can see that the systems change over time, should we think in terms of "Christianities" rather than of "Christianity"? When the perspective of study is strictly historical, it might well be helpful to speak in the plural when characterizing the faith of the Church in different times. But because one system can interact with others, it is plain that the systems are sufficiently coherent that they are not only sensible to one another, but also capable of changing one another. Christianity, it appears clearly, is not only a particular system, but also a tradition of systems, as in the case of the most enduring religions that continue to play their part in contemporary culture.

Skilful theologians have sought to use the power of tradition to influence the systems of their day. In the period after World War II, a movement called Neo-Orthodoxy gained currency in the West. It sought a middle way between the "Social Gospel" and Fundamentalism with an appeal to the classic foundations of the past.

NEO-ORTHODOXY

Neo-Orthodoxy had its beginnings in the work of Karl Barth; Dietrich Bonhoeffer and Rudolf Bultmann were among its ablest defenders. All of them were prominent throughout their careers before World War II, but post-War theology (particularly American theology)—in its attempt to find an international orientation which would serve as a biblically oriented model of human suffering and the hope of redemption—made their perspective into a principle of ecumenical discussion. Barth, Bonhoeffer, and Bultmann became standard points of reference in academic theology in the United States, and the influence of their work on the curricula of theological seminaries would be difficult to overestimate.

Within the perspective of Neo-Orthodoxy, the reading of salvation history into the Bible is essential. This interpretation follows the perspective of Augustine, the founder of global history in Christianity. Before Augustine, there was no coherent argument to the effect that human events were both consequential in their revelation of God and meaningfully sequential in their unfolding. Those are the conditions *sine qua non* of salvation history: divine meaning must attach to specific events and to the relationship among events for history to be redemptive. The argument of Neo-Orthodoxy was that history was the category of all humanity's redemption.

One of the proponents of Neo-Orthodoxy, Reinhold Niebuhr, developed a prayer whose appeal was so great, medieval attribution has often been claimed for it. Its resonance with the system identified with the Middle Ages is striking:

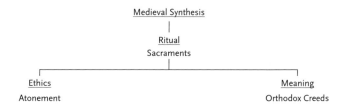

Yet the prayer, for all its simplicity, conveys the sense of an organic whole and reflects much of the systems of Christianity we have encountered: the themes of witness in the manner of Jesus (see Chapter 1), of the hope of salvation in the presence of God (see Chapter 2), of the need to atone for sin (see Chapter 3), of the central importance of faith (see Chapter 4), and of the connection between integrity and Christ (see Chapter 5).

REINHOLD NIEBUHR'S "SERENITY PRAYER"

God grant me grace with serenity to accept the things that cannot
  be changed;
Courage to change the things that should be changed;
and wisdom to distinguish the one from the other.
Living one day at a time;
Enjoying one moment at a time;
Accepting hardships as a pathway to peace;
Taking, as Jesus did, this sinful world as it is, not as I would have it;
Trusting that You will make all things right if I surrender to
  Your Will;
So that I may be reasonably happy in this life
and supremely happy with You forever in the next.

Successful theologies negotiate the relations among Christian systems of the past in their adaptation into new forms and embody the claim of believers that a single orientation toward God is the common substance of the Church in every age.

Yet even as Barth's Neo-Orthodoxy was making its way into a privileged position theologically, another voice gave new direction to the practice of Christianity. In 1911, Evelyn Underhill published *Mysticism: A Study of the Nature and Development of Man's Spiritual Consciousness*. At the time at which she wrote, Enlightenment skepticism had long made any claim of direct knowledge of God appear irrational. But she insisted:

> To be a mystic is simply to participate here and now in that real and eternal life; in the fullest, deepest sense which is possible to man. It is to share, as a free and conscious agent—not a servant, but a son—in the joyous travail of the Universe: its mighty onward sweep through pain and glory towards its home in God. This gift of "sonship," this power of free co-operation in the world-process, is man's greatest honour.

By rooting her description in an understanding of developing consciousness, Underhill provided a basis for seeing spirituality as an intrinsically human endeavor. To her, the path of consciousness had been mapped out by earlier mystics, including Angela of Foligno, Julian of Norwich, Mechthild of Magdeburg, Catherine of Genoa, Catherine of Siena, Margery Kempe, Teresa of Ávila, Rose of Lima, and Jeanne-Marie Guyon. She did not merely master the literature involved, but found a way to describe a common pattern of her definition of mystical experience.

EVELYN UNDERHILL'S ANALYSIS OF MYSTICISM

Evelyn Underhill set out a repeated pattern among mystical practitioners, a structure of consciousness that could be analyzed and replicated. Writing from the point of view of the soul, she said:

It began by the awakening within the self of a new and embryonic consciousness: a consciousness of divine reality, as opposed to the illusory sense-world in which she was immersed. Humbled, awed by the august possibilities then revealed to her, that self retreated into the "cell of self-knowledge" and there laboured to adjust herself to the Eternal Order which she had perceived, stripped herself of all that opposed it, disciplined her energies, purified the organs of sense. Remade in accordance with her intuitions of reality, the "eternal hearing and seeing were revealed in her." She opened her eyes upon a world still natural, but no longer illusory; since it was perceived to be illuminated by the Uncreated Light. She knew then the beauty, the majesty, the divinity of the living World of Becoming which holds in its meshes every living thing. She had transcended the narrow rhythm by which common men perceive but one of its many aspects, escaped the machine-made universe presented by the cinematograph of sense, and participated in the "great life of the All." Reality came forth to her, since her eyes were cleansed to see It, not from some strange far-off and spiritual country, but gently, from the very heart of things. Thus lifted to a new level, she began again her ceaseless work of growth: and because by the cleansing of the senses she had learned to see the reality which is shadowed by the sense-world, she now, by the cleansing of her will, sought to draw nearer to

> that Eternal Will, that Being, which life, the World of Becoming, manifests and serves. Thus, by the surrender of her selfhood in its wholeness, the perfecting of her love, she slid from Becoming to Being, and found her true life hidden in God.

Underhill did not restrict her attention to women mystics, but included them with men. The steady repetition of the pattern she discovered added force to her argument that a feature of human consciousness was involved in spirituality, and at the same time she promoted the growing view that women, no less than men, had a place in the spiritual life. She became a force both for the concept of a spirituality that transcends a particular time and place and for the role of women in religion. Male writers after her built on her work without adequately acknowledging her pioneering role, and by the time the ordination of women was discussed at the World Council of Churches in 1948 and later became a reality in many churches, her influence had largely been forgotten.

Basic to Underhill's approach was the understanding that people enjoy their kinship to God on the basis of consciousness, not considerations such as gender or sexuality. Without intending to, she was delineating a fresh iteration of the Christian system:

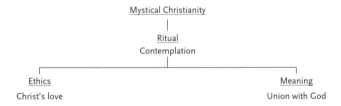

Even those who supported Evelyn Underhill sometimes expressed unease with her wide-seeking horizon; she sought out the wisdom of consciousness among Muslim and Platonist practitioners, for example, not only in Christian texts. This kind of interest in spirituality is sometimes described as post-Christian among observers, because it clearly does loosen the ties to doctrine that have typified many Christian systems. But in using Christ as a lens for the experience of God, it may be that Underhill's approach to mysticism anticipated a fresh development in the unfolding tradition of Christian religious systems.

FURTHER READING

Barth, Karl (1956) *Church Dogmatics*, vol. 1: *The Doctrine of the Word of God* (eds G. W. Bromiley and T. F. Torrance; translators G. T. Thomson and Harold Knight) (Edinburgh: T. & T. Clark).

Bell, Catherine (2009) *Ritual. Perspectives and Dimensions* (New York: Oxford University Press).

Fox, Matthew (1991) *Creation Spirituality. Liberating Gifts for the Peoples of the Earth* (San Francisco: Harper).

Geertz, Clifford (1993) *The Interpretation of Cultures. Selected Essays* (London: Fontana).

Jenkins, Philip (2007) *God's Continent. Christianity, Islam, and Europe's Religious Crisis* (Oxford: Oxford University Press).

Niebuhr, Reinhold (2013) *Moral Man and Immoral Society. A Study in Ethics and Politics* (Louisville, KY: Westminster John Knox Press).

Underhill, Evelyn (1911) *Mysticism. A Study in the Nature and Development of Man's Spiritual Consciousness* (London: Methuen).

GLOSSARY

Alaric (370–410 CE) became king of the Visigoths in 395 CE. Denied a position within the Roman Empire, Alaric undertook a series of campaigns in Greece and Italy, at that time a vulnerable region for Constantinople, and successfully besieged Rome itself between 409 and 410 CE. He died during a campaign to invade North Africa.

Allegory, which derives from the Greek term *allegoria*, refers to the description of one thing by means of reference to another. In particular, mythical or spiritual realities might be described metaphorically in terms of perceptible phenomena, physical or historical.

Anchorite or anchoress denotes a hermit who, in order to achieve seclusion, withdraws from the world. Such a withdrawn person (*anakhoretes* in Greek) typically sought seclusion in cells built in close proximity to churches, a practice that became widespread in the Middle Ages.

Angel means "messenger" and derives from the Greek term *angelos* (equivalent to the Hebrew *malakh*). Israelites conceived of God as reigning in his heavenly Kingdom, surrounded by angelic courtiers. He responded to prayer by dispatching an angel, and the messenger might be experienced visually, in audible words, or as interior illumination.

Anselm of Canterbury (1033–1109) was a Benedictine abbot who became archbishop of Canterbury in 1093 and pioneered the "ransom theory," according to which God receives the recompense for human sin, with Christ's death the gift of a blameless and noble life in exchange for the guilt of others.

Apocrypha   literally means "hidden" in Greek. Between 390 and 405 CE, St. Jerome translated the Old Testament into Latin, and he spoke of works in the Septuagint that had no Hebrew exemplars as "apocrypha." During the Reformation, the term was taken by Protestants to mean that such works were not canonical.

Apostle   derives from the Greek term *apostolos*, and means someone who is sent, an agent. Because Jesus sent some of his disciples to be his personal representatives and instructed them to act as he did, apostles became the highest authorities in his movement.

Arian   refers to the teaching of Arius (250–336 CE), a North African priest active in Alexandria. In opposition to the view held by the Council of Nicea in 325 CE, Arius maintained that God the Father needs to be seen as prior to the Son in time and in majesty, so that monotheism could be clearly maintained. Dismissed as a heretic, his works have not survived, but, during the Enlightenment, thinkers such as Isaac Newton championed Arian theology.

Askesis   means "exercise" or "training" in Greek. The root of ascetic practice in the Christian tradition is not self-abnegation for its own sake, but training on behalf of the values of the faith.

The Assumption of the Virgin Mary   was declared as infallible doctrine by Pope Pius XII in 1950. He stated that she was assumed body and soul into heaven. Orthodoxy refers to the Dormition of the God-bearer, and the content of the belief is comparable, although with a greater variety of conceptions.

Athanasius   (298–373 CE) set himself in opposition to Arius and as Patriarch of Alexandria insisted on the fully divine nature of Christ and his co-eternity with the Father. He became the chief exponent of Trinitarian theology.

Augustine   (354–430 CE), Catholic bishop of Hippo, taught that humanity currently lived in the thousand-year rule of the saints, the millennium predicted in the Revelation of John (20:4). This age of dawning power, released in flesh by Jesus and conveyed by the Church, simply awaits the full transition into the city of God.

Baptism   for John the Baptist was not a once for all act. As in Judaism as a whole, purification was a routine requirement, and people could return to John many times. In the practice of the early Church, believers felt that they received the Spirit of God when they were immersed in the name of Jesus. That conviction emerged *after* the resurrection and stemmed from the belief that Jesus was alive at the right hand of God and able to dispense divine Spirit (see Acts 2:33).

Barnabas, recognized as an apostle in the book of Acts, was a leader of the early Church who had been born in Cyprus from the line of the Levites, the priestly clan of ancient Israel. He contributed to the movement at the earliest stage and after his death a second-century source, *The Epistle of Barnabas*, applied typology in his name to the Old Testament in order to set out the significance of Jesus.

Benedict of Nursia (480–547 CE) led an exemplary life as a hermit, and his repute for sanctity and miraculous powers brought many followers. He crafted a rule of life, setting out principles of living in community. His Rule became standard in the West, and his monastery at Monte Cassino in Italy emerged as a touchstone of the virtues of obedience and moderation.

Bishop (Greek *episkopos*) initially referred to the secular role of a manager or overseer in any community and was applied to those in congregations who had charge of communal resources. Once those resources grew with Constantine's recognition of Christianity as a legitimate religion, the role of bishop naturally became preeminent.

Blandina was a young woman slave. With the other martyrs of Lyons, she was tortured and killed at the order of Roman magistrates in 177 CE for her refusal to recant her faith. The long and graphic description of her suffering became a classic in early Christian literature.

Calvin, Jean (1509–64) emerged as the most influential leader of the Reformation. Although he was active in several cities, Geneva became his focus. Under his leadership it was known as the Protestant Athens and used as a city of refuge for European sympathizers. Calvin established a carefully orchestrated structure of pastors, teachers, elders, and deacons, and he also developed the most searching theology of divine Providence that Christianity has ever known.

Canon means "measure" or "standard" in Greek and came to refer among Orthodox Catholic believers to those works that both derived from apostolic teaching and were used throughout the Church.

Catechumen   simply means "someone who is taught" in Greek, but it came to refer to a person who prepared himself for baptism within the Church by an extensive process of study, fasting, and prayer.

The **Cathars**   were the target of a Crusade in 1209, proclaimed by Pope Innocent III, for such sins as claiming that Mary Magdalene was the mistress of Jesus and that the papacy did not represent the spiritual authority of the Church.

Catholic   comes from the Greek term *katholikos* that means "universal" (literally, "through the whole" or "for the whole"). Catholics defined the emerging faith in terms of belief and practice throughout the Church in the world as they knew it.

Christ   derives from the word *khristos* in Greek and means someone who is anointed. The equivalent in Hebrew is *mashiach,* which gives us the English word Messiah. In the Hebrew Bible, a person might be anointed with olive oil as a routine matter, to cleanse the skin or care for a wound, and scented oil was a luxury. But one might also be anointed as a king, a prophet, or a priest, so the term itself came to imply religious status.

Christology   refers to the science (*logos* in Greek) of what makes Jesus the Christ.

Church   is a truncated English pronunciation of *ekklesia* in Greek, a term that originally meant an assembly of people "called out" (from the verb *ekkaleo*) for a public meeting. Use of the term reflects the Christian conception that a congregation of believers was not merely a like-minded group of people, but a community of those who heard and listened to the call of God.

Creed   see *Sumbolon.*

Crusade   as preached by Pope Urban II in 1095, called for warriors who would literally bear the sign of the cross on their chests during their journey to Jerusalem, as pilgrim cross-bearers (*croisés* in French, crusaders in English).

Cyprian of Carthage   (200–258 CE) was the leading bishop of his age. In a deeply divisive controversy in North Africa over whether priests who did not oppose Roman persecutors at every opportunity were worthy of continuing in ministry, Cyprian taught that priests were empowered by Christ, not their own virtue.

Cyril of Alexandria   (376–444 CE) led the churches in his influential city and championed a sacrificial theology, according to which Christ's death on the cross was a sacrifice that God required for himself.

Darby, John Nelson   (1800–82) was an Anglo-Irish priest who pursued a pre-millenarian reading of 1 Thessalonians 4:17 in an apocalyptic scenario inspired by the Revelation. Darby added an innovation: the prediction of seven years of tribulation at the hands of the antichrist for those who remained on earth. His theology of "dispensations," successive epochs of God's relationship to humanity, became widespread.

Deacon   (from the Greek word for a servant, *diakonos*) came to be an ancillary role in relation to the increasingly managerial bishop in the period after Constantine.

Deconstruction   insists that meaning only occurs in the mind of the interpreter, by means of engagement with the text.

Deism   reached its height as a religious movement during the eighteenth century in England, although it enjoyed prominent supporters in America and France. Its confidence that reason and faith could be combined in theology derives from the Enlightenment and still informs Liberal Christianity.

Descartes, René   (1596–1650), a signal Enlightenment contributor to geometry and philosophy, saw cognition as the center of being in his famous dictum, "Cogito, ergo sum" (I think, therefore I am).

Diaspora   literally means "dispersion" in Greek, and refers to how Jews since the time of the Babylonian invasion of their land in 587 BCE lived all over the civilized world, adopting many new languages and cultures even as they maintained their identity as Israel.

Dionysius Exiguus   set out tables in 525 CE for the dates of Easter in the Julian calendar which had been promulgated in 45 BCE. In so doing, he established a Christian scheme of chronology ("BC" and "AD") that is still in use.

Disciple   at base means "student," someone who studies with a rabbi, and derives from the Latin translation of the term *talmid* ("learner") in Aramaic.

Dominic (Guzmán)   (1170–1221) founded the Order of Preachers, commonly called the Dominicans. Preaching was designed to combat heresy, and the Order became associated with the Inquisition in Spain. Dominic's own emphasis on intellectual argument provided the precedent for Dominican involvement in education, and the Order is known for promoting the widespread use of the Rosary.

Dostoevsky, Fyodor (1821–81), a Russian novelist, explored the religious, political, and moral problems posed by human suffering.

Edwards, Jonathan (1703–58), a Congregationalist minister in New England, pursued his Calvinist theology in a way that made it consistent both with Enlightenment conceptions of reason and the movements of religious revival that he nurtured.

Epiphany means "manifestation" in Greek and refers to Christ's manifestation of God on earth.

Erasmus of Rotterdam (1466–1536), a Dutch priest and scholar, was the foremost humanist in northern Europe and a leader in a call for the reform of the Church.

Ethics determine how a person should behave, whether in public or in private.

Francis of Assisi (1181–1226) founded the Order of Friars Minor and related communities in order to take up the preaching of Christ as reflected in the Gospels. The Franciscans became known for their embrace of apostolic poverty as a living example of Christ's teaching.

Franklin, Benjamin (1706–90) was a founding father of the American Revolution, a key figure in the relationship between the new nation and France, and an inventor and philosopher. He espoused the Deism fashionable in his time.

Fundamentalism is a late Protestant movement which articulated the alleged "Fundamentals" of Christianity: biblical "inerrancy;" the birth of Jesus from a biological virgin; Jesus' performance of miracles that defy natural law; Jesus' atonement for the sins of others by shedding his blood on the cross; Jesus' resurrection in the same body in which he died, and his return to earth in that body at the end of days. The Presbyterian General Assembly of 1910 articulated these teachings as "essential and necessary."

Gnosticism is a modern term for a movement that thrived from the late first century until the end of the fourth century CE. Gnosticism sought a single integrating insight (*gnosis,* which means "knowledge" in Greek) into the divine world.

God-fearers (*theophoboumenoi*) were Gentiles who accepted the God of Israel without practicing all the commandments specifically related to Israel in the Torah.

Gospel in English represents the Greek term *euangelion* (hence the adjective "evangelical"), which refers to news of victory in battle. The equivalent of *besorta'* in Aramaic, it was applied by Jesus to his preaching of God's kingdom (see Mark 1:14–15) and later to the message about Jesus in the four Gospels and related literature.

Gregory of Nyssa, the younger brother of Basil the Great, bishop of Caesarea, lived between 330 and 394 CE. Gregory's letter, *That there are not three Gods*, represents a breakthrough in Trinitarian thought in the fourth century.

Guibert of Nogent, a Benedictine abbot, wrote *Dei gesta per Francos* (1108), an account of the first Crusade.

Gutiérrez, Gustavo (1928–), a Peruvian priest who now teaches in the United States at Notre Dame University, gave Liberation Theology its name as well as its dialectical emphasis on biblical imperative and social justice. His meeting with Pope Francis in September 2013 has appeared to some observers to constitute a major change from the negative assessment of Liberation Theology under John Paul II and Benedict XVI.

Hegel, G. W. F. (1770–1831) developed a view of history according to which ideals met in the shape of a thesis and an antithesis and produced a synthesis that then moved on to successive dialectical encounters.

Hermit designates a person who lives a life of contemplative seclusion in the wilderness (*eremos* in Greek, a term also rendered as "desert").

Herod the Great (73 BCE–4 BCE) was a successful client king of Rome who ruled Judea, Samaria, Galilee, as well as to the east of the Dead Sea. His son, Herod Antipas, is the Herod most referred to in the Gospels

Hume, David (1711–76) was a Scottish philosopher who pressed the claims of reason over those of faith in the way the contributed to the sense during the later Enlightenment of a cleavage between the two.

Ignatius of Antioch, bishop of that city, refused, when he was denounced as a Christian, to offer sacrifice to the Roman gods or to acknowledge the emperor as divine. He was sentenced to die in Rome by being fed to wild animals, a form of punishment that enabled the Roman Empire to satisfy the demands of its justice and to provide entertainment all at once. Letters he wrote early in the second century in the period leading up to his martyrdom became classics of early Christian literature.

Imitatio Christi   refers to the ethic of following Jesus' example so closely as to walk in his footsteps (see 1 Peter 2:21) and therefore inherit his glory.

Indulgences   reflect the power of the Church to reduce the temporal punishment for a sin. Although a sin can be forgiven only by God, the consequences that follow from a sin, whether during life or in purgatory, may be shortened. During the Reformation Protestants criticized the papacy for a system of indulgences that seemed to them corrupt.

Irenaeus, born in Asia Minor, became bishop of Lyons after the persecution of 177 CE. His writings championed a conception of the Church as catholic, that is, universal, grounded in the Scriptures of Israel as well as the four Gospels and in a recognition of the physical world as God's creation.

Isaac, the son of Abraham and of Sarah, was born after a divine promise despite the advanced age of his parents (Genesis 17). God tested Abraham and ordered him to sacrifice Isaac; only the redemption of the beloved son by means of a ram permitted him to live (Genesis 22). Early Christian interpreters saw Isaac as a type of Christ.

James   is named as the first of Jesus' four brothers in Mark 6:3. The number of children attributed to Mary and Joseph suggests that James was Joseph's son by a previous marriage. Both the New Testament and the Jewish historian Josephus attest James' great reputation in Jerusalem, as a result of his dedication to the Temple. Until his death in 62 CE James was the most influential teacher within the fledgling Church.

Jansen, Cornelius   (1585–1638) was a Dutch theologian who held out the prospect of a reconciliation between Catholicism and Protestantism by means of his work on Augustine's teaching on grace, free will, and predestination. Suspicion that he conceded too much to Protestantism resulted in opposition from the Jesuits, and finally from the Vatican.

The **Jerusalem Council** is the name given to the meeting of apostles and other teachers in Jerusalem in 46 CE. It determined that Gentiles might be baptized into the faith without requiring them to keep the covenant of circumcision. A later meeting, in 52 CE, insisted that such non-Jewish believers should nonetheless abstain from eating food sacrificed to idols and animals that had been suffocated rather than bled out before slaughter, and from fornication.

John Cassian (360–435 CE) was a monk and scholar who traveled widely and developed close contacts with many leaders in the Church. In 415 CE he established a monastery in Marseilles that brought the traditions and practices of Egypt to the West, a service even more effectively performed by his writings.

Josephus was a leader in the Jewish insurrection against Rome who changed sides and wrote influential histories under imperial protection. His writings, especially *The Jewish War* (75 CE) and *Antiquities of the Jews* (93 CE) constitute major sources for Christian history in its earliest period.

Julius II, Pope (1443–1513) greatly enhanced the Vatican by beginning work on a new St Peter's Basilica and commissioning Michelangelo to paint the ceiling of the Sistine Chapel. These efforts went hand in hand with extending the practice of indulgences that brought in revenue, as well as a series of military and political campaigns that were designed to strengthen the position of the Vatican as a court.

Justin Martyr (100–165 CE) pioneered the Christian Platonism that dominated the theology of the Church until the Middle Ages, made the Prophets of Israel into the agents of true philosophy, and Christ the source of prophetic inspiration.

Kant, Immanuel (1724–1804) developed the most comprehensive account in his time of the levels of cognition in which human beings operate. He believed that pure reason, reflection on phenomena, and the practical reason that leads to ethical judgments are related but quite different kinds of cognition.

The **Kingdom of God** in Aramaic refers to the promise that people will finally come to realize divine justice and peace in all that they do. People will put into action with one another the righteousness they see in God. So the Kingdom is a matter of vision, of perceiving God at work both in the present and in the future, but it is also a matter of ethics.

LaHaye, Tim   is the creator of the best-selling "Left Behind" series of the 1990s and 2000s. LaHaye portrays the Revelation of John as a forecast of how a new temple must be built in Jerusalem in order to provoke a war that will bring human civilization to an end before Jesus' return in glory.

Leo X, Pope   (1475–1521) succeeded Julius II and continued many of his policies. His sale of indulgences provoked the criticism of Martin Luther, whom Leo condemned in his bull, *Exsurge Domine* (1520).

Liberal Theology   refers to the pursuit of truth on the Enlightenment understanding that reason and faith work together for the same or similar aims.

Locke, John   (1632–1704) espoused the classic Deist conception of the agreement of faith and reason, and applied that conviction to his understanding of the Bible and his analysis of government.

Logos   means "word" in Greek, with the sense of the animating logic of a term, rather than its syllables. Stoic philosophers prior to Christianity had spoken of the *logos* as the design of creation and the ideal plan of the social world, and the idea was taken up by the Jewish Philosopher Philo of Alexandria, and then in the Gospel according to John.

Loisy, Alfred   (1857–1940) applied the methods of Liberal theology within the Roman Catholic Church, where his movement was known as modernism.

The **Lord's Prayer** or **Paternoster**   is the signature prayer of Jesus, which he taught to his disciples and which stands as a virtually universal practice of Christianity. The basic model of the Lord's Prayer consists of calling God father, confessing that his name should be sanctified and that his kingdom should come, and then asking for daily bread, forgiveness, and not to be brought to the test.

Luther, Martin   (1483–1546) provided the moving force of the Reformation with his insistence that God's grace alone, rather than any human institution, offered the prospect of salvation. His influence as a writer, translator, hymnist, and disputant are unmatched in the history of the Church.

Macrina   (330–79 CE), sister of Basil the Great and Gregory of Nyssa (two of the three theologians known as the Cappadocian Fathers), lived an ascetical life in a community she founded. Her brother Gregory wrote of her discipline, which embodied the ways of purification (*katharsis*), contemplation (*theoria*), and union with God (*theosis*).

Martyr   is a term that simply means "witness" (*martus*) in Greek. In the context of Roman persecution, when magistrates might require believers to commit idolatry by sacrificing to the emperor's image and overtly to curse Christ, the word came to refer to the willingness to die for one's faith.

Marx, Karl   (1818–83) applied Hegel's dialectical reasoning to economic conditions and saw the disturbances that affected Europe in 1848 as a sign that the new class of workers produced by the Industrial Revolution would see in a permanent order of collective ownership and individual freedom.

Mass   derives from the closing words of the Eucharist when it is celebrated in Latin: *Ite, missa est* ("Go: it is dismissal"). Its use to refer to the entire service is an example of naming the whole from one of its parts.

Meaning   tells participants in a religious system *why* they do what they do and even why they exist.

Milton, John   (1608–74), best known as the author of *Paradise Lost*, was a Puritan polemicist who served in the Commonwealth of Oliver Cromwell, justified the beheading of Charles I, and produced an early argument for the role of individual conscience in determining religious belief.

Mishnah   means "repetition" in Hebrew and derives from how disciples of a rabbi learned to repeat his teaching in oral form until they had memorized and mastered it. By the end of the second century CE, the teachings of many rabbis were gathered into the collection called the Mishnah (capitalized), the basic document of Rabbinic Judaism.

Monk   is a shortened, Anglicized form of the Greek term "solitary" (*monakhos*). In their ascetic practice, the earliest monks took on the austerities to live in the wilderness, concentrating on the tasks of prayer and meditation.

Montesquieu, Charles de Secondat, baron de   (1689–1755) pioneered a conception of the separate and balancing branches of government in order to promote justice as a human aim.

The **New Testament**   consists of twenty-seven writings that include four Gospels, letters (of Paul and other writers), and a combination of apocalyptic writings and documents intended for the Church at large. In aggregate, they are accorded privilege in Christianity as showing how the prophecies of the Old Testament have been realized in Christ.

Niebuhr, Reinhold (1892–1971) was an American theologian who promoted "Christian realism," an acknowledgement of human sinfulness in the tradition of Augustine and Calvin that also endorses the hope of revelation in history.

The **Old Testament**, whether in its Hebrew form or in the Greek translation called the Septuagint, consists of the scriptures of Israel as recognized in the first century.

Origen   of Alexandria (185–254 CE) was the most powerful Christian thinker of his time. His pioneered the compared study of texts of the Old Testament, while his commentaries and sermons illustrate the development of a conscious method of interpretation. His most characteristic work, *On First Principles*, is the earliest comprehensive Christian philosophy extant. His *Against Celsus* is a classic work of apologetics, and his contribution to the theory and practice of prayer (represented in the classic source of meditation edited by Basil the Great in the fourth century, the *Philokalia*) is unparalleled.

Pascal, Blaise   (1623–62) was a French mathematician and philosopher who explored the relationship between faith and reason. He died before he could complete his work, but it was published posthumously as *Pensées* ("Thoughts").

Paul of Tarsus   became, second to Jesus, the most influential teacher in Christianity. But he only emerged with that stature after his death in 64 CE, owing to the influence of his letters. They formed a core collection within the New Testament and appealed to the increasingly non-Jewish constituency of Christianity, because Paul insisted that Gentiles and Israelites enjoyed the same status in God's sight and within the Church.

Pentecost   was originally the Greek name of a Jewish festival, but it is associated in Christianity with the endowment of Jesus' followers with the Spirit of God. Seven weeks after the close of the entire festival of Passover and Unleavened Bread came the feast called Weeks or Pentecost (which in Greek, refers to the period of fifty days that was involved).

Perpetua   was a Roman noblewoman who was martyred in Carthage in 203 CE. Her account of her visions and faith captured the imagination of early Christians.

Peter means "rock" in Greek. Jesus applied that nickname (in the form of its Aramaic equivalent, *Keypha'*) to his early disciple, Simon, one of his closest followers.

Pharisees held that an oral Torah also needed to be followed alongside the written Law. The oral Torah also derived from Moses in their view, but could only be accessed through the teachings of the Pharisees themselves. Because they held to additional regulations as necessary to make an Israelite pure, they came to be called "Separatists," the probable meaning of the term "Pharisee."

Plato the most famous disciple of Socrates, lived between 428 BCE and 347 BCE and founded an academy in Athens. His conception that reality as we know it is an imitation of ideal forms became a staple of philosophy after his time.

Pope comes from the word *papa*, a term of respect for the bishop of Rome, and another term for "patriarch," the senior bishop of a major metropolitan area.

Pre-millenialist expectations conceive of Christ coming in judgment *before* the millennium of the saints described in Revelation 20:1–6. A post-millenialist view sees the definitive judgment of Christ as coming after the millennium.

Priest derives from Greek *presbuteros*, which means "elder." (In both Hebrew and in Greek, a different term, *kohen* and *hiereus* respectively, referred to the agent of literal sacrifice.) In the first churches, as in synagogues, the elder was expected to give order to the local congregation according to the traditions known to him.

Purgatory, as its name suggests, is a place of purification. Understood to occur after death, in Origen's teaching, purgatory prepares believers for their eventual enjoyment of heaven.

Purity refers in religious systems to the state of being that God intends for a part of the created order. If an object, person, or another living thing transgresses that state, purification becomes necessary.

"Q" abbreviates the German word (*Quelle*), which means source, and refers to a collection of Jesus' sayings in the Gospels.

Rabbi is an address that a student would use of a teacher in Aramaic, meaning "my great one." Although its meaning was generic during the first century, by the end of the second century

Rabbis emerged in a more specialized way as the successors of the Pharisees who claimed that their oral Torah was conveyed in the Mishnah.

The **Rapture** is the name applied to 1 Thessalonians 4:17, where Paul says that "the dead in Christ will arise first, then we who are alive, remaining, will be snatched up together with them in clouds to meet the Lord in the air." Some Christian thinkers from the seventeenth century conceived of the "rapture," the millennium of the Apocalypse, and the second coming of Christ as all combined in a single moment of divine judgment.

Rauschenbusch, Walter (1861–1918) was an American theologian who helped to found the movement known as the "Social Gospel." In his conception, the Kingdom of God as taught by Jesus was a transformative principle that moved human history in the direction of divine love.

Recapitulation (from Latin *recapitulatio*) refers to the teaching championed by Irenaeus that Christ sums up the whole of human experience, taking it through the sin of Adam to the end that was always willed by God.

Redemption is the process by which God chooses not to require what is due to him, for example a sacrificial victim or punishment for sin. Instead he redeems the person who might have been killed or punished by accepting another offering. In Christian thought, the offering *par excellence* is the death of Christ as recollected in the Eucharist.

Relics are the remains of saints. Any part of a holy person's body, having been transformed by God's Spirit, can convey sanctity and the power of healing. The Second Council of Nicea in 787 CE set out that all churches should incorporate relics.

Religious systems combine social relations and activities—ritual, ethics, and meaning—that exist independently, but put them together into a mutually reinforcing system.

Renan, Ernest (1823–92) was a French theologian devoted to the study of Christian origins as well as of Judaism and Islam. His writing on Jesus (1863) earned him the condemnation of being a "European blasphemer" by Pope Pius IX because of Renan's insistence on describing his subject in historical terms.

Restoration (from Greek *apokatastasis*) is a teaching espoused by Origen, according to which God's will is to bring all of human experience back to the promise at the beginning of creation and then to realize that promise.

Ritual   is a set of communal actions in which each participant needs to understand the role to be played and the sequence of acts to be followed.

Romanticism   represents an emphasis upon lyric poetry and its associated forms, together with a regard for sensibility and imagination in their relation to reason.

Romero, Óscar   (1917–80), archbishop of San Salvador, supported efforts to protect the poor of his nation and opposed their oppression by its government. He called on the United States to cease military aid to his country and on soldiers to disobey orders to murder their own people. He was killed by an assassin while he said Mass in a hospital chapel.

Rosary   refers to the use of prayer beads. Roman Catholicism has systematized the use of such beads in the Rosary, a precisely sequenced cycle of the "Mysteries" of Christ's birth, ministry, death, resurrection, and ascension. In the Rosary, alongside the Paternoster, the "Hail Mary" is said: "Hail Mary, full of grace, the Lord is with thee; blessed art thou amongst women, and blessed is the fruit of thy womb, Jesus. Holy Mary, Mother of God, pray for us sinners, now and at the hour of our death. Amen."

Rousseau, Jean-Jacques   (1712–78) became a leading theorist of the social contract that bound human beings together, and pursued the thought of how they should manage their interests and appetites.

Sadducees   controlled proceedings in the Temple in Jerusalem. They were an hereditary priesthood among privileged families, allegedly derived from Zadok (hence their name in the Greek Gospels).

Schleiermacher, F. D. E.   (1768–1834) developed a keen sense of the connection between faith and imagination, and also championed the Gospel according to John as providing a greater sense of the historical Jesus than the other Gospels.

Septuagint   refers to the Scriptures of Israel in Greek, named after the seventy translators who allegedly produced the rendering. Major teachers in Judaism accepted this Jewish Bible as authoritative, although it included works in Greek that had no counterpart in the Hebrew Bible that the Rabbis canonized. Additional works of this kind, known as apocryphal, include the Wisdom of Solomon and the books of Maccabees.

Simeon Stylites   (390–459 CE) was an ascetic who lived for thirty-seven years on a platform atop a pillar near Aleppo.

The **Social Gospel**   is the early twentieth-century movement of Liberal Theology that saw the Kingdom of God as a force that was realized by means of political and economic progress.

Son of God   is a term used in the Hebrew Bible for a person who is brought into a close relationship to God. So, in Psalm 2:7 God is portrayed as saying, "You are my son; this day I have begotten you." Jesus saw himself in relation to God in this way and thought of his followers as being God's sons or children. After the time of Jesus, in the fourth century, creeds saw Jesus' sonship as implying that his being—as contrasted to other humans'—was fully divine.

Structuralism   posits that in the development of language and literature, certain essentials of discourse could be discerned, and that without such discernment, interpretation was impossible.

Sumbolon   in Greek etymologically refers to a throwing together and conveys how a word, phrase, sign, or statement can invoke a larger set of ideas or relations. The Christian *sumbolon* as used at baptism came to be called a *credo* in Latin, which means "I believe." The English term "creed" developed from this usage.

Synagogues   were "gatherings" of people as the term *sunagoge* means in Greek, but the term referred increasingly to buildings, whether converted private homes or purpose-built.

Synoptic   is a description of the Gospels according to Matthew, Mark, and Luke, which can be "seen together" (the meaning of the term in Greek) because they are comparable in wording, content, and order.

The **Ten Commandments**   appear in the Scriptures of Israel in Exodus 20 and Deuteronomy 5, and in Christianity they are interpreted so as to apply to humanity at large.

Theodosius I   (347–95 CE) was the last Roman emperor to rule over both the eastern and western regions of the imperium. He issued edicts that made Trinitarian Christianity the official religion of the Roman Empire.

Thomas Aquinas   (1225–74) became preeminent among scholastic theologians and sought a synthesis between Aristotle's philosophy, with its focus on logical sequence in nature, and revealed faith. His innovation brought condemnation both during his life and posthumously, but his teaching was endorsed by Pope Leo XIII in 1879 as the definitive exposition of Catholic faith.

Torah means "guidance" in Hebrew, and refers to the revelation given to Moses in the period between the exodus and Israelite settlement in the land of Canaan. Rendered "law" (*nomos*) in Greek, the Torah reached into the matter of common behavior, the regulation of sacrifice, and the maintenance of that standard of purity that was expected of Israel as a sacrificial community.

Trajan, emperor of Rome between 98 and 117 CE, recognized that Christians could not be treated simply as Jews. But he also stated in correspondence with one of his governors (Pliny, in 111 CE), that they should not be persecuted just because they were Christians; they could be required to recognize the gods of Rome and then released.

Transubstantiation, as taught by Thomas Aquinas, holds that in the Eucharist the "accidents" or outward characteristics of bread and wine remain the same, while their "substance" or essential quality becomes the body and blood of Christ.

Typology in Christian interpretation is a combination of Plato's philosophy of ideal forms and the prophetic claim that God fulfills his signs of promise. As it is applied to the Old Testament, the result is to see "types" of Christ and believers in the narrative concerning Israel, as well as in overt prophecy.

Underhill, Evelyn (1875–1941) was a prolific writer, an influential theologian, and a pioneering figure in the study and practice of mysticism. In addition, her scholarship on the history of liturgy anticipated the Ecumenical reform of worship in the twentieth century.

The **Westminster Confession** of 1646 set out Puritan principles for the Church of Scotland and the Church of England that applied Calvinist principles to those nations. The Confession continues to serve as a reference for Congregationalist, Presbyterian, and Reformed churches.

BIBLIOGRAPHY

REFERENCE SOURCES

ANSELM

See Brown, David (2004) "Anselm on Atonement," *The Cambridge Companion to Anselm*; Cambridge Companions (eds Brian Davies and Brian Leftow) (Cambridge: Cambridge University Press): 279–302.

AQIBA

See Finkelstein, Louis (1970) *Akiba. Scholar, Saint and Martyr* (New York: Atheneum).

AQUINAS, THOMAS

See Aquinas, Thomas (2006) *Summa theologiæ. Latin text and English translation, introductions, notes, appendices, and glossaries* (Cambridge and New York: Cambridge University Press): III.75.

ARNAUD-AMAURY

See Vaux-de-Cernay, Pierre des (1998) *The History of the Albigensian Crusade. Peter of les Vaux-de-Cerny's Historia Albigensis* (trs. W. A. and M. D. Sibly) (Woodbridge: Boydell): 51 (paragraph 91).

ATHANASIUS

For the Festal letter of Athanasius, see Camplani, Alberto (ed. and tr.) (2003) *Lettere festali. Atanasio di Alessandria: Letture cristiane del primo millennio* 34 (Milan: Paoline).

For his *Life of Anthony*, see Vivian, Tim, Athanassakis, Apostolos N., and Greer, Rowan A. (eds and trs.) (2003) *The Life of Antony* (Kalamazoo, MI: Cistercian Publications).

For *On the Incarnation*, see Meijering, E. P. (ed. and tr.) (1989) *Athanasius: De Incarnatione Verbi, Einleitung, Übersetzung, Kommentar*, with J. C. N. van Winden (Amsterdam: Gieben).

AUGUSTINE

McCracken, G. E., Green, W. M., Wiesen, D. S., Levine, P., Sanford, E. M., and Green, W. M. (eds and trs.) (1957–72) *Augustine: City of God*: Loeb Classical Library (Cambridge, MA: Harvard University Press).

Hill, Edmund and Rotelle, John E. (eds and trs) (1991) *Sermons (51–94) on the New Testament* (Brooklyn: New City Press).

BABYLONIAN TALMUD

See Epstein, I. (ed.) (1935–48) *The Babylonian Talmud* (London: Soncino).

BASIL THE GREAT

For the *Philokalia*, see Bingaman, Brock and Nassif, Bradley (eds) (2012) *The Philokalia. A Classic Text of Orthodox Spirituality* (New York: Oxford University Press): 31.

BONHOEFFER, DIETRICH

See Lawrence, Joel (2010) *Bonhoeffer. A Guide for the Perplexed* (London and New York: T & T Clark).

BULTMANN, RUDOLF

See Fergusson, David (1992) *Bultmann, Outstanding Christian Thinkers* (London: Chapman).

CALVIN, JEAN

For his *The Institutes of the Christian Religion* and the *Ecclesiastical Ordinances*, see Kuyper, Abraham and Boonstra, Harry (eds and trs.) (2009) *Our Worship*,

Calvin Institute of Christian Worship Liturgical studies (Grand Rapids, MI: William B. Eerdmans Pub. Co.).

CASSIAN, JOHN

See Stewart, Columba (1998) *Cassian the Monk* (New York: Oxford University Press).

CHRONICLE OF CHÂLONS-SUR-MARNE (1794)

See Kramnick, Isaac (1995) *The Portable Enlightenment Reader* (New York: Penguin Books).

CLEMENT VI

For his *Unigenitus*, see Wood, Diana (1989) *Clement VI. The Pontificate and Ideas of an Avignon Pope* (Cambridge: Cambridge University Press): 32–3.

CONGREGATION OF THE DOCTRINE OF THE FAITH

See http://www.vatican.va/roman_curia/congregations/cfaith/documents/rc_con_cfaith_doc_19850311_notif-boff_en.html (accessed 8 March 2014).

COUNCIL OF CHALCEDON

See Jenkins, Kelly and Jenkins, Philip (2010) *Jesus Wars. How Four Patriarchs, Three Queens, and Two Emperors Decided What Christians Would Believe for the Next 1,500 Years* (New York: HarperOne).

CRANMER, THOMAS

For his *Book of Common Prayer*, see Church of England (1901) *The First and Second Prayerbooks of King Edward the Sixth* (London: Dent).

CREED OF CHALCEDON

See Kelly, J. N. D. (2006) *Early Christian Creeds* (London: Continuum).

CYPRIAN

See Lang, Bernhard (1997) *Sacred Games. A History of Christian Worship* (New Haven, CT: Yale University Press): 91–100.

CYRIL OF ALEXANDRIA

For the *Pascal Homilies*, see Amidon, Philip R. (ed. and tr.) (2009) *Cyril of Alexandria. Festal letters 1–12*, Fathers of the Church (Washington: Catholic University of America Press).

DARBY, JOHN NELSON

See Darby, John Nelson (1839) *Notes on the Book of Revelation. To Assist Enquirers in Searching into that Book* (London: Central Tract).

DARWIN, CHARLES

See Darwin, Charles (1959) *On the Origin of Species by Means of Natural Selection* (London: Murray).

DESCARTES, RENÉ

For his "Discourse on Method," see Weissman, David (ed.) (1996) *Discourse on the Method and Meditations on First Philosophy* (New Haven, CT: Yale University Press).

DIONYSIUS EXIGUUS

See Declerq, Georges (2000) *Anno Domini. The Origins of the Christian Era* (Turnhout: Brepols).

DOSTOEVSKY, FYODOR

For *The Brothers Karamazov*, see Dostoevsky, Fyodor (2008) *The Karamazov Brothers* (tr. Ignat Avsey) (New York: Oxford University Press).

EDICT OF MILAN

See Creed, J. L. (ed. and tr.) (1984) *Lactantius: De Mortibus Persecutorum*: Oxford Early Christian Texts (Oxford: Clarendon).

EDWARDS, JONATHAN

For his *Treatise concerning Religious Affections* (1746), see Miller, Perry (ed.) (1957–) *The Works of Jonathan Edwards* (New Haven, CT: Yale University Press).

EPISTLE OF BARNABAS

See Ehrman, Bart D. (ed. and tr.) (2003) *The Apostolic Fathers*: Loeb Classical Library (Cambridge, MA: Harvard University Press)

ERASMUS, DESIDERIUS

For *Against Barbarians, Handbook of the Christian Soldier, In Praise of Folly*, and *Julius Excluded from Heaven,* see Rummel, Erika (ed. and tr.) (1990) *The Erasmus Reader* (Toronto: University of Toronto Press).

For *Novum Instrumentum*, see Erasmus, Desiderius (1516) *Novum Instrumentum omne* (Basel: Froben).

For "On contempt of the World," see Hyma, Albert (ed. and tr.) (1930) *The Youth of Erasmus* (Ann Arbor, MI: University of Michigan Press).

EUSEBIUS

See Lake, Kirsopp (ed. and tr.) (1980) *Eusebius: The Ecclesiastical History*: Loeb Classical Library (Cambridge, MA: Harvard University Press).

For his *Praise of Constantine*, see Drake, H. A. (1978) *In Praise of Constantine. A Historical Study and New Translation of Eusebius' Tricennial Orations* (Berkeley, CA: University of California Press).

FIRST VATICAN COUNCIL

For the doctrine of papal infallibility (1870), see Küng, Hans (1983) *Infallible? An Inquiry* (tr. Edward Quinn) (Garden City, NY: Doubleday).

FRANCIS OF ASSISI, ST.

For his "Canticle of the Sun," see Armstrong, Regis J., Hellmann, J.A. Wayne, and Short, William J. (eds and trs) (1999–2001) *Francis of Assisi: Early Documents* (New York: New City Press).

FRANKLIN, BENJAMIN

For his letter to Ezra Stiles, see Kramnick, Isaac (1995)*The Portable Enlightenment Reader* (New York: Penguin Books).

FULCHER OF CHARTRES

See Peters, Edward (1998) *The First Crusade. The Chronicle of Fulcher of Chartres and Other Source Materials* (Philadelphia, PA: University of Pennsylvania).

GALILEO

For "A Dialogue between the Two Great Systems of the World," see Drake, Stillman (1978) *Galileo at Work: His Scientific Biography* (Chicago: University of Chicago Press).

GERARDO DI BORGO SAN DONNINO

For the *Introduction to the Eternal Gospel*, see Baird, Joseph L., Baglivi, Giuseppe, and Kane, John Robert (eds) (1986) *The Chronicle of Salimbene de Adam*, Medieval and Renaissance Texts and Studies 40 (Binghamton, NY: Medieval and Renaissance Texts and Studies).

GOSPEL ACCORDING TO THE HEBREWS

See Schneemelcher, Wilhelm (ed. and tr.) (2003) *New Testament Apocrypha* (Louisville, KY: Westminster John Knox).

GOSPEL ACCORDING TO THOMAS

See Robinson, James M. (1990) *The Nag Hammadi Library in English* (San Franscico: Harper).

GREGORY I (GREGORY THE GREAT)

For his *Commentary on Job*, see Adriaen, Marc (ed.) (1979–85) *S. Gregorii Magni Moralia in Job*: Corpus Christianorum (Turnholt: Brepols): 31.

For his *Forty Gospel Homilies*, see Hurst, Dom David (1990) *Gregory the Great: Forty Gospel Homilies Translated from the Latin*, Cistercian Studies Series 123 (Kalamazoo, MI: Cistercian Publications).

GREGORY OF NYSSA

For his *Life of Macrina*, see Corrigan, Kevin (ed. and tr.) (1997) *The Life of Saint Macrina*, Peregrina Translation Series 12 (Toronto: Peregrina).

For *That there are not three Gods*, see Maspero, Giulio (ed. and tr.) (2007) *Trinity and Man: Gregory of Nyssa's* Ad Ablabium: *Supplements to Vigiliae Christianae* 86 (Leiden: Brill).

For his weeping whenever he saw an icon of Isaac, see Nikolasch, Franz (1969) "Zur Ikonographie des Widders von Gen 22," *Vigiliae Christianae* 23 (Leiden: Brill): 197–223.

GUIBERT OF NOGENT

See Levine, Robert (1997) *The Deeds of God through the Franks: A Translation of Guibert de Nogent's Gesta Dei per Francos* (Rochester, NY: Boydell).

GUTIÉRREZ, GUSTAVO

See Gutiérrez, Gustavo (1970) "Notes for a Theology of Liberation," *Theological Studies* 31: 243–61.

HEGEL, GEORG WILHELM FRIEDRICH

See Dickey, Laurence and Nisbet, H. B. (1999) *G. W. F. Hegel: Political Writings*, Cambridge Texts in the History of Political Thought (Cambridge: Cambridge University Press).

HENRY VIII

For *The Defense of the Seven Sacraments against Martin Luther*, see Gent, T. W. (ed. and tr.) (1766) *Assertio Septem Sacramentorum : or, A Defence of the Seven Sacraments, against Martin Luther. By Henry the Eighth, King of England, France, and Ireland. To which are adjoined, his Epistle to the Pope. The Oration of Mr. John Clark, (Orator to his Majesty) on the Delivery of this Book to his Holiness. And The Pope's Answer to the Oration. As also, the Pope's Bull, by which his Holiness was pleased to bestow upon that king (for composing this Book) that most illustrious, splendid, and most Christian-Like title of Defender of the faith* (Dublin: Byrn).
For his Six Articles, see Adams, George Burton and Stephens, H. Morse (eds) (1939) *Select Documents of English Constitutional History* (New York: Macmillan).

HILLEL

See Hadas-Lebel, Mireille (1999) *Hillel. Un Sage au Temps de Jésus* (Paris: Albin Michel).

HIPPOLYTUS

See Easton, Burton Scott (ed. and tr.) (1934) *The Apostolic Tradition of Hippolytus* (Cambridge: Cambridge University Press).

HUME

For his "Essay on Miracles" (1748), see Millican, Peter (ed.) (2002) *Reading Hume on Human Understanding* (Oxford: Clarendon Press).

IGNATIUS OF ANTIOCH

See Ignatius, *Epistle to the Smyrnaeans* 8 in Ehrman, Bart D. (ed. and tr.) (2003) *The Apostolic Fathers*: Loeb Classical Library (Cambridge: Harvard University Press).

IGNATIUS LOYOLA

For his *Spiritual Exercises*, see Ganss, George E. (1992) *The Spiritual Exercises of Saint Ignatius. A Translation and Commentary* (Chicago: Loyola Press).

IRENAEUS

For the *Refutation of False Knowledge* and *Against Heresies*, see Rousseau, Adelin (ed. and tr.) (1984) *Contre les heresies. Dénonciation et réfutation de la gnose au nom menteur. Par Irénée de Lyon* (Paris: Les Éditions du Cerf).

JAMES VI AND I

For "The True Law of Free Monarchies," see Fischlin, Daniel and Fortier, Mark (eds) (1996) *James I: The True Law of Free Monarchies and Basilikon Doron* (Toronto: Centre for Reformation and Renaissance Studies).

JEFFERSON, THOMAS

See Walters, Kerry (2011) *Revolutionary Deists. Early America's Rational Infidels* (Amherst, NY: Prometheus Books).

JEROME

For the *Liber de Viris Illustribus*, see Claudia Barthold (ed. and tr.) (2011) *Hieronymus: De viris illustribus: Berühmte Männer* (Mülheim: Carthusianus Verlag).

JOSEPHUS

Thackeray, H. St. J., Marcus, Ralph, Wikgren, Allen, and Feldman, Louis H. (eds. and trs.) (1930–65) *Josephus: Jewish Antiquities*: Loeb Classical Library (Cambridge, MA: Harvard University Press).

Thackeray, H. St. J. (ed. and tr.) (1997) *Josephus: The Jewish War*: Loeb Classical Library (Cambridge, MA: Harvard University Press).

JUBILEES

See Charlesworth, James H. (ed.) (1983–85) *The Old Testament Pseudepigrapha* (Garden City, NY: Doubleday).

JUSTIN MARTYR

See Falls, Thomas B. (ed. and tr.) (2013) *Saint Justin Martyr: The First Apology, the Second Apology, Dialogue with Trypho, Exhortation to the Greeks, Discourse to the Greeks, the Monarchy, or the rule of God* (Baltimore, MD: Project Muse).

KADDISH

See Scherman, Nosson (1991) *The Kaddish Prayer: A New Translation with a Commentary Anthologized from Talmudic, Midrashic and Rabbinic Sources* (Brooklyn, NY: Mesorah).

KANT, IMMANUEL

For "What is Enlightenment?," see Kant, Immanuel (1784) "Beantwortung der Frage: Was ist Aufklärung?," *Berlinische Monatsschrift* (December): 481–94.

KIERKEGAARD, SØREN

See Lowrie, Walter (ed. and tr.) (1941) *Fear and Trembling and Sickness unto Death* (Princeton, NJ: Princeton University Press).

KING, MARTIN LUTHER

For his "Letter from Birmingham Jail," see King, Jr., Martin Luther (1963) "The Negro is Your Brother," *Atlantic Monthly* 212: 2.

LAHAYE, TIM

For the Left Behind series, see LaHaye, Tim and Jenkins, Jerry B. (2011) *Are We Living in the End Times?* (Carol Stream, IL: Tyndale House).

LEO X

For *Exsurge Domine*, see Hutten, Ulrich von (ed.) (1520) *Bulla decimi Leonis, contra errores Martini Lutheri* (Strassburg: Schott).

LINDSEY, HAL

See Lindsey, Hal with Carlson, C. C. (1970) *The Late, Great Planet Earth* (Grand Rapids, MI: Zondervan).

LOCKE, JOHN

For his "Two Treatises on Government" and his *Letters concerning Toleration*, see Shapiro, Ian (ed.) (2003) *Two Treatises of Government and a Letter concerning Toleration: John Locke* (New Haven, CT: Yale University Press).

LOISY, ALFRED

See Sainte Suzanne, Raymond de Boyer de (1968) *Alfred Loisy: Entre la foi et l'incroyance* (Paris: Éditions du Centurion).

LUTHER, MARTIN

See Brecht, Martin (1990) *Martin Luther. Shaping and Defining the Reformation* (Minneapolis, MN: Augsburg Fortress).

For his *Against the Murdering, Thieving Hordes of Peasants* and *Secular Authority*, see Höpfl, Harro (ed. and tr.) (1991) *Luther and Calvin on Secular Authority*, Cambridge Texts in the History of Political Thought (Cambridge: Cambridge University Press).

For his *Against the Rioting Peasants*, see Helfferich, Tryntje (ed. and tr.) (2013) *Martin Luther: On the Freedom of a Christian, with Related Texts* (Indianapolis, IN: Hackett).

For his translation of the Bible, see, Luther, Martin (tr.) (1534) *Biblia, das ist, die gantze Heilige Schrifft Deutsche* (Wittenberg: Hans Lufft).

For his "Disputation on the Power and Efficacy of Indulgences" and *To the Christian Nobility of the German Nation*, see Dillenberger, John (ed.) (1961) *Martin Luther. Selections from his Writings*, Anchor Books (Garden City, NY: Doubleday).

MARTYRDOM OF PERPETUA

See Hefferman, Thomas J. (ed.) (2012) *The Passion of Perpetua and Felicity* (New York: Oxford University Press).

MARX, KARL

For Marx on the plight of peasants in the Mosel region (1842), see Draper, Hal (1977) *Karl Marx's Theory of Revolution* (London: Monthly Review Press): 84–5.

MATHER, COTTON

See Weber, Eugen (1999) *Apocalypses: Prophecies, Cults, and Millennial Beliefs through the Ages* (Cambridge, MA: Harvard University Press): 170.

MATHER, INCREASE

See Weber, Eugen (1999) *Apocalypses: Prophecies, Cults, and Millennial Beliefs through the Ages* (Cambridge, MA: Harvard University Press): 170.

MILTON, JOHN

For *Paradise Lost*, see Dyson, A. E. and Lovelock, Julian (eds) (1973) *Milton: Paradise Lost* (London: Macmillan).

For "The Tenure of Kings and Magistrates," see Dzelzainis, Martin (ed.) (1991) *Milton: Political Writings*, Cambridge Texts in the History of Political Thought (Cambridge and New York: Cambridge University Press).

MISHNAH

See Neusner, Jacob (ed.) (1988) *The Mishnah. A New Translation* (New Haven, CT: Yale University Press).

MONTESQUIEU, CHARLES

See Neaud, Pierrette M. (1995) *Montesquieu: Biographie, étude de l'œuvre* (Paris : Albin Michel).

For his letter of 1721, see Kramnick, Isaac (1995) *The Portable Enlightenment Reader* (New York: Penguin Books).

NEWTON, SIR ISAAC

For his *Mathematical Principles of Natural Philosophy*, see Kramnick, Isaac (1995) *The Portable Enlightenment Reader* (New York: Penguin Books).

NICEAN CREED

See Kelly, J. N. D. (2006) *Early Christian Creeds* (London: Continuum).

NIEBUHR, REINHOLD

For his "Serenity Prayer," see Sifton, Elisabeth (2003) *The Serenity Prayer: Faith and Politics in Times of Peace and War* (New York: Norton).

ORDERIC VITALIS

See Riley-Smith, Jonathan (1986) *The First Crusade and the Idea of Crusading*, The Middle Ages Series (Philadelphia, PA: University of Pennsylvania): 28.

ORIGEN

For *Against Celsus*, see Chadwick, Henry (ed. and tr.) (1980) *Origen: Contra Celsum* (New York: Cambridge University Press).

For the *Apology*, see Scheck, Thomas P. (2012) *Apology for Origen. On the Falsification of the Books of Origen*, Fathers of the Church (Washington, DC: Catholic University of America Press).

For his *Commentary on John*, see Heine, Ronald E. (1969) *Origen: Commentary on the Gospel according to John*, Fathers of the Church (Washington, DC: Catholic University of America Press).

For *On First Principles*, see G. W. Butterworth (ed. and tr.) (1966) *Origen: On First Principles* (New York: Harper and Row).

For the *Philokalia*, see Palmer, G. E. H., Sherrard, Philip, and Ware, Kallistos (eds. and trs.) (1979) *The Philokalia. The Complete Text* (Boston: Faber and Faber). See also Junod, Éric (2006) *Origène: Philocalie 21–27: Sur le libre arbitre*, Sources chrétiennes 226 (Paris: Éditions du Cerf).

PASCAL

For his *Pensées*, see Sellier, Philippe (ed.) (1991) *Blaise Pascal: Pensées* (Paris: Bordas).

PAUL III

For the *Licet ab initio*, see Peters, Edward (1988) *Inquisition* (New York: Free Press).

PAUL IV

For the *Index of Prohibited Books*, see Peters, Edward (1988) *Inquisition* (New York: Free Press).

PETER THE VENERABLE

See Cohen, Jeremy (2004) *Sanctifying the Name of God: Jewish Martyrs and Jewish Memories of the First Crusade* (Philadelphia, PA: University of Pennsylvania): 3–4.

PIUS IX

For the doctrine of the Immaculate Conception (1854), see Küng, Hans (1983) *Infallible? An Inquiry* (tr. Edward Quinn) (Garden City, NY: Doubleday).

PIUS XII

For the doctrine of the Assumption of the Blessed Virgin Mary (1950), see Gentle, Judith Marie and Fastiggi, Robert L. (eds) (2009) *De Maria numquam satis: The Significance of the Catholic Doctrines on the Blessed Virgin Mary for All People* (Lanham, MD: University Press of America).

POPE, ALEXANDER

For his "An Essay on Man," see Pope, Alexander (1734) *An Essay on Man* (London: Wilford).

RAUSCHENBUSCH, WALTER

For his "Social Gospel," see Evans, Christopher H. (2001) *The Social Gospel Today* (Louisville, KY: Westminster John Knox Press).

RAYMOND D'AGUILERS

See Asbridge, Thomas (2004) *The First Crusade. A New History* (Oxford: Oxford University Press): 316.

RENAN, ERNEST

See Renan, Ernest (1863) *Vie de Jésus* (Paris: Lévy)

ROMERO, ÓSCAR

For his pastoral letter, see Kellogg Institute at the Notre Dame University: http://kellogg.nd.edu/romero/Biography.htm (accessed 8 March 2014).

ROUSSEAU, JEAN-JACQUES

See Dent, Nicholas (2005) *Rousseau*, Routledge Philosophers (London: Routledge).
For *Emile, or on Education*, see Rousseau, Jean-Jacques (1979) *Emile or On education* (tr. Allan Bloom) (New York: Basic Books).

SCHLEIERMACHER, F. D. E.

See Brandt, Richard B. (1968) *The Philosophy of Schleiermacher: The Development of his Theory of Scientific Knowledge* (New York: Greenwood): 84–5.

SCOFIELD, CYRUS

For his Reference Bible, see Scofield, Cyrus I. (1909) *The Holy Bible Containing the Old and New Testaments: Authorized King James Version with a New System of Connected Topical References* (New York: Oxford University Press).

TANG STELE (EIGHTH CENTURY)

See Keevak, Michael (2008) *The Story of a Stele. China's Nestorian Monument and its Reception in the West, 1625–1916* (Hong Kong: Hong Kong University Press).

THEODOROS THE GREAT ASCETIC, ST.

For the *Philokalia*, see Palmer, G. E. H., Sherrard, Philip, and Ware, Kallistos (eds and trs.) (1979) *The Philokalia. The Complete Text* (Boston: Faber and Faber). See also Junod, Éric (2006) *Origène: Philocalie 21–27: Sur le libre arbitre*, Sources chrétiennes 226 (Paris: Éditions du Cerf).

THEODOSIUS

See Boyd, William K. (1905) *The Ecclesiastical Edicts of the Theodosian Code* (New York: Columbia University Press).

THOMAS À KEMPIS

See Thomas à Kempis (1998) *The Imitation of Christ in Four Books* (ed. and tr. Joseph N. Tylenda) (New York: Vintage).

TRAJAN

For the Letter of the Emperor Trajan to Pliny, see Stout, Selatie Edgar (1962) *Plinius, Epistulae: A Critical Edition* (Bloomington, IN: Indiana University Press).

URBAN II

See Peters, Edward (1998) *The First Crusade: The Chronicle of Fulcher of Chartres and Other Source Materials* (Philadelphia, PA: University of Pennsylvania).

ZWINGLI, ULRICH

See Potter, G. R. (1976) *Zwingli* (Cambridge: Cambridge University Press).

INDEX